When William Rose,
	Stephen Vincent and I Were Young

When William Rose,

BOOKS BY LAURA BENÉT

    The Boy Shelley
    Famous American Humorists
    Famous American Poets
    Famous New England Authors
    Famous Poets for Young People
    Famous Storytellers for Young People
    Stanley, Invincible Explorer
    The Mystery of Emily Dickinson
    When William Rose, Stephen Vincent and I Were Young

Stephen Vincent and I Were Young

LAURA BENÉT

ILLUSTRATED WITH PHOTOGRAPHS

DODD, MEAD & COMPANY · NEW YORK

Photographs courtesy of Laura Benét except for the picture on page 43, courtesy of Moravian College, Bethlehem, Pennsylvania

Copyright © 1976 by Laura Benét
All rights reserved
No part of this book may be reproduced in any form
without permission in writing from the publisher

Library of Congress Cataloging in Publication Data

Benét, Laura.
   When William Rose, Stephen Vincent and I were young.

   Includes index.
   SUMMARY: An author reminisces about her childhood and that of her two famous brothers.
    1. Benét, Laura—Biography—Youth—Juvenile literature. 2. Benét, William Rose, 1886–1950—Biography—Youth—Juvenile literature. 3. Benét, Stephen Vincent, 1898–1943—Biography—Youth—Juvenile literature. [1. Benét, Laura. 2. Benét, William Rose, 1886–1950. 3. Benét, Stephen Vincent, 1898–1943. 4. Authors, American] I. Title.
PS3503.E528Z52   810′.9′0052[B]   [920]   75-38366   ISBN 0-396-07289-5

FOR
>	*Rosemary Casey*
who has done so much for me,
without whose wonderful help
I could not have written this book
With love and deep gratitude,
>	THE AUTHOR

Contents

1.	*First Things*	*1*
2.	*Two Dear Households*	*9*
3.	*Sorrento*	*16*
4.	*Frankford Arsenal*	*23*
5.	*Bethlehem*	*39*
6.	*Enter Stephen*	*55*
7.	*Buffalo*	*65*
8.	*Watervliet Arsenal*	*71*
9.	*Benicia Arsenal*	*85*
	Index	*109*

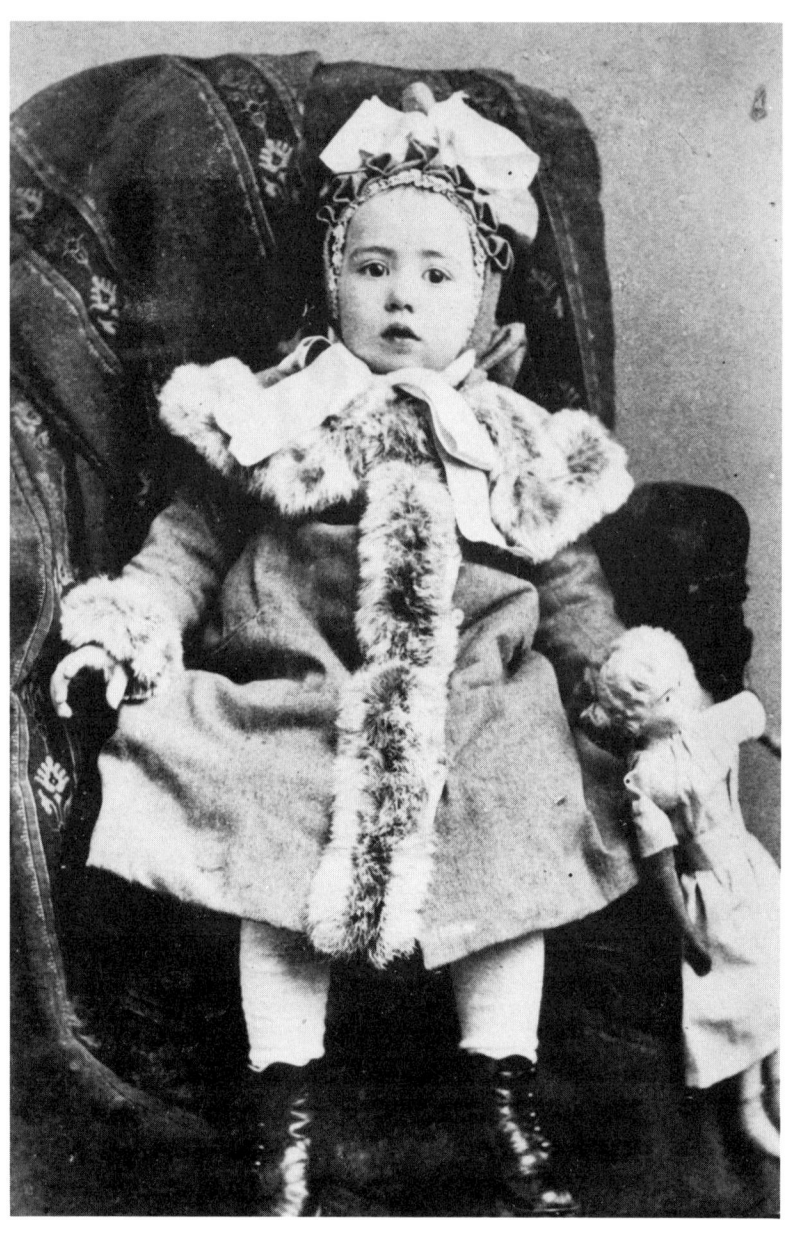

Laura Benét at one and a half years of age

CHAPTER ONE

First Things

In the early years, there were just the two of us, William Rose (Willie) and I, Laura. The first home that I remember is the Army house at Springfield Arsenal in Massachusetts. We were small children when we moved there from Fort Hamilton, Brooklyn, in November, 1886. Willie was not quite a year old, and I was two and a half.

Our father, James Walker Benét, a second lieutenant in the Ordnance Corps, had just been transferred from the artillery when he was assigned to this post. He was six feet tall, with brown hair, and had brown eyes that could dance with mischief. He had regular features; his face was intellectual, with a quizzical expression.

Our mother, named Frances, had light-brown hair, blue eyes, a wild-rose complexion, and the sweetest and kindest of faces. Her surname had been Rose, and a rose she was in every sense

James Walker Benét as a Cadet at West Point

of the word. She was always called Fanny or Fan. Before they met in 1882 at Fortress Monroe, Virginia, where Mother was vacationing with her mother and sister, Father told the friend who had invited them that he could not like any girl by the name of "Fanny."

Frances Rose, May 13, 1882

"You will fall in love with *this* Fanny," the friend said. And he did.

Mother, for her part, did not care for James as a name. So she always called her husband "Jack."

Father got on famously with General Buffington, commandant of the Arsenal, though other officers did not, being afraid of him. General Buffington knew our grandfather, General Stephen Vincent Benét, who was Chief of Ordnance. Dim as my picture of the general has become, the word "Belchertown" brings it before me. I journeyed with Father and Mother to this Massachusetts town when I was about three, with the Buffingtons and their daughter Eliza, who was a year older than I. Here the memory ends. What we did, why we went, is a blank. Whether it was for the day or an overnight excursion I cannot recall—only the magic word "Belchertown" remains.

Even at the age of three, motion was a part of my nature. In Springfield it was indulged. One of my very early recollections I owe to Eliza Buffington. She had a tricycle that she rode constantly, and she let me stand on the rear bar behind her, my arms around her neck. Back and forth we went all over the parade ground, for she was not ungenerous. She shared with me another treasure she possessed. She had a doll with rubbers, microscopic in size, that fitted on over its shoes. I have never seen any like them since.

Our house, known as "quarters," was pleasant and roomy, with a front porch. This porch was always a favorite place to sit. One day when we had been living there a year or two, Mother peeped from the front door and saw Willie and me seated on the steps, one in a sunbonnet, one in a piqué hat. I, who did not read as yet, held a book open and was diligently pretending to impart its contents to my little brother. Presently she heard the book slapped shut with a bang as I explained, "The rest is in French. You wouldn't understand it." Mother had to hurry away to hide her laughter.

Father had an extraordinary memory and was pleased to discover that his first born had inherited it and could repeat correctly everything of importance or unimportance that she was told.

One drawer in a small parlor table contained many photographs of Mother as a young girl. The first had been labeled by Father "Where the brook and river meet," and, "This one," he often said, holding up another, "is your mother just budding into womanhood." Then he produced a third. "Here she is in the first flush of youth and beauty."

I thought this a wonderful game and soon had all the descriptions by heart. One morning Mother had an early caller. She was not quite ready and, before changing her dress upstairs, called down to me to talk to Mrs. So-and-So and tell her that she, Mother, would be down in a few minutes.

In a friendly mood, I entered the parlor. What better amusement for the visitor than the precious pictures? I dumped out the drawer and began expounding the appropriate legend for each one to the caller, much to her amusement. Mother arrived just in time to stem the tide of description.

"She must have thought us a most peculiar family," commented Father, later. "It was all your fault," said Mother.

We had a nurse while we were at Springfield Arsenal called Annie Montanya. She loved the small brother, for he was a gentle lamb who never did anything wrong. She called Willie her blue-eyed boy, but she was not popular with me or I with her. I would seize the chance when I was alone to rush to the nearby quarters of our friends, the Clark family, where Mrs. Clark often read aloud one of my favorite, very sad stories about a boy named Leslie.

"Oh, Mith Clark, Mith Clark, read Leslie quick, read Leslie quick, Annie coming soon," I would beg, fearful of being hauled away before the story was done.

Annie used to be filled with wrath because I did not obey her. "Them Spanish eyes," she would say when I disobediently danced up and down on the pavement, my brown hair flying, for I never had curls. "Bad Annie," I would chant. "Bad Annie, dirty Annie."

My grandmother, my mother's mother, Mary Lee Rose or "Ammah," as we called her, was my champion and fortress. Her I would have obeyed if I had been asked to put my hand in the fire. She lived with us until I was five—benign, calm, adorable, and adored by me and everyone. Her life had not been an easy one, as she had had many trials and little money.

My other grandmother, Laura Walker Benét, for whom I was called "Laura," was much gratified at having a namesake. She had money of her own, left by her father, the prosperous owner of a plantation in Richmond, Kentucky. She bought all my clothes; my baby underwear was made by nuns in a Washington convent, and I wore white dresses for some time. Think of the wash, all done by hand!

Grandmother Benét taught me to read at five, and I learned quickly. When I had exhausted the primer, I was presented with *Uncle Tom's Cabin*. I remember that little red-and-white book perfectly.

Father's only brother, Laurence Benét, a bachelor, was for years engaged in business in Paris. Uncle Larry was a charming man with a beard like silk that I loved to twine with my fingers. On his visits home every year or two he would bring his only niece and nephew the most enchanting French toys that ever graced any nursery. One of Willie's gifts was a man on a velocipede (the forerunner of the bicycle) which you could wind up and watch in awe as it wheeled about the room.

Laura Benét at four years of age—"them Spanish eyes"

Mrs. Very, a friend of our Grandmother Benét, must have helped my uncle in the selection of my dolls, of which I had many. The French baby dolls were darling, tiny twins dressed exactly alike, with bonnets—one in pink and one in blue. They slept in a little bed together and were too delicate to be picked up constantly. Then there was the cherished "long baby," Margaret, who had two faces, a smiling one and a crying one. A string pulled in her side effected the transformation. Bangs of brown hair on her head fitted both faces. She could suck a bottle of milk (made from a little cologne and water) *by herself*. She slept in a bassinet and she wore long clothes and French "barrow coats" and small close caps like a little Parisian child.

But Mimi, the French doll that *talked*, was the pride and delight of my life. She was carefully housed in Mother's room and only brought out on state occasions such as birthdays and Christmas. She had lace robes and the softest blonde curls, said "Mama" and "Papa" alternately, and kicked her wax legs when you wound her up with a key.

One birthday when we had had our usual gathering of small friends, Ammah bore Mimi downstairs to show her accomplishments. But on that occasion Mimi was a spoiled child and would not perform for anyone. She remained stubbornly dumb and silent, no matter how Ammah wound her. Finally Ammah said sadly, "This is too bad, children. Something has gone wrong with her works," and carrying Mimi upstairs again, she laid her on a bed in an unoccupied room on the floor just beneath the maids' room.

That night Mary and Maggie roused the household, declaring that they heard ghosts. But it was only little Mimi who had erratically consented to murmur "Mama" and "Papa" and kick her legs at two o'clock in the morning.

CHAPTER TWO

Two Dear Households

WE spent about three years at Springfield Arsenal and then we went to Washington, D.C. Grandfather Benét's term of office as Chief of Ordnance was drawing to a close, and he wanted his son with him to share his duties before he retired.

We were to live with our grandparents in the tall, spacious house at 1717 I Street and to have the front of the third story entirely to ourselves. Farragut Square was nearby for us to play in. Here Willie exercised his new velocipede, of which he was very proud, and I wheeled my dolls up and down the paths. Willie was a gentle child who could entertain himself by the hour, but I needed active occupation and as I grew older I pined for friends and fresh adventures.

Our first visit to Washington proved a hectic chapter. The climate never agreed with me and I had continual colds. Then poor little Willie came down with typhoid fever. Mother, who

William Rose Benét, taken at Washington, D.C., about 1888

had just had an operation, had planned, on her recovery, to have some pretty dresses made and enjoy a taste of the social life of Washington. Instead she was faced with the desperate illness of this child whom the doctor and nurse thought they could not save.

Our grandparents' friends were most solicitous and very kind. Among the gifts they sent to divert Willie later on was a china dog that survived for many years. Upon receiving it, Willie remarked, "He has a gentle face."

Also there were many families of small china animals received. Every night during his convalescence, Willie's command to Mother was, "Pack boxes," and the animal families were wound up in tissue paper and deposited in their several boxes, from which small fingers unpacked them in the morning. Also, there was a box of blocks always called the "Legron blocks" because a Mrs. Legron gave them to him.

Willie had remarkable tenacity and pulled through. He completed his recovery the following summer in Maine, where he was wheeled around in an express wagon until he grew strong enough to run about himself.

Meanwhile, what of me? I had been hurried off to Ammah's new home in Carlisle, Pennsylvania, at once, lest I, too, develop the fever. Ammah no longer lived with us but resided with her half-brother, Montgomery Mahon, known to us as Uncle Mont, and her elder daughter, Elizabeth Neill Rose, our "Auntie." Auntie was nervous and high strung but a devoted daughter and a wonderful teacher of small children. She had charge of the primary and intermediate pupils at Metzger Institute in Carlisle.

Next to the school and separated from it by a garden with a boxwood hedge, old Mr. Metzger had built a house of numerous gables for himself. But as he had long since been gathered to his fathers and that unique house was for rent, Ammah, Auntie, and Uncle Mont had rented it and moved in. A pleasant front porch opened upon a hallway with two large rooms on either side, the East Parlor and the West Parlor. The East Parlor was, for the most part, reserved for company; the West Parlor (which contained the preserve closet) was for utilitarian occupations, though it did have a piano.

Upstairs were three delightful bedrooms, one quite large, as well as a huge bathroom and a small attic. Of course, when we came to visit with Mother there was much doubling up to be done, and Auntie often slept at the school. Because the school was so close she was able to come home every day for lunch at which she often amused us by telling funny stories of her scholars.

Uncle Mont was connected with the Pennsylvania Railroad, and every weekday morning after an early breakfast he walked to the station and took the train for Harrisburg and his office. He returned each night at dinner time, and after dinner we enjoyed his company. Willie and I loved nothing better than to settle in his room and hear his stories about the Chinaman who was employed to wash his clothes.

A widower who had lost his young wife early, Uncle Mont never remarried, though all Auntie's friends fell for him. He had one son my age who visited him every summer but lived with an aunt the rest of the year. Uncle Mont was devoted to Ammah, whom he called "Sister," and had been only too glad to cast in his lot with her and her daughter.

Uncle Mont had many of the qualities of an actor and was a capital mimic. For years Willie believed firmly in the existence of the dog that barked under the dining room table—and of the baby who yelled upstairs, at which Uncle Mont would say to him reproachfully, "You've waked the baby!"

The house was nearly set on fire once through one of Uncle Mont's pranks. He manufactured a man out of bolster and pillow, dressed it in his clothes, and laid it in his bed while he went out for the evening. A friend of Auntie who was visiting went to turn down his bed and, thinking a burglar was concealed there, nearly dropped the lighted oil lamp she carried. Once when our fussy Great-aunt Kate was visiting, Uncle Mont left his old straw hat on the hall table for Auntie, marked "Lizzie from Aunt Kate."

Ammah for many years had a cook named Mollie who had a son named Nat. Nat brought Willie turtles from the creek and rode him about on his back. After a time there was a second maid named Jane who was rather eccentric. "Trusty Jane is now quite ready for Kirkbrides," wrote Uncle Mont once, referring to the local insane asylum. In another letter, he said of the family cat, "Alice got nothing at all for Christmas except abuse from your aunt and a bite on the ear from the tom cat next door. I," he continued, "received 35 handsome presents including a liver pad," which was an old-fashioned remedy. His imagination was fertile and he would have been inimitable on the stage.

Diagonally across to the left from Ammah's house in Carlisle lived Marianne Moore with her mother and her brother, Warner. She was a quiet child—very much of a "clam," I thought. She was not writing poetry yet, to my knowledge, but was very clever with her hands, doing tatting and embroidery. She loved cats, of which the Moores had a number. "I was sitting," I once heard her say, "one day on the porch with the elder kittens."

It was while on an early visit to Ammah in Carlisle that I met my loyal friend of a lifetime, Ellinor Blaine Hays. My grandmother took me, soon after my arrival, to the green house diagonally across the street to the right and rang the bell. When Mrs. Hays came in person to answer it, a little girl with short dark hair was clinging to her skirts. When asked if she would like to go over and play with Mrs. Rose's little girl, Honey, as she was always called, breathed "Yes." She was too young for school; so was I. We took to each other at once and played happily together. She was more practical than I and had her feet on the earth, while my mind was set on ideal conditions, as the following story shows.

One night some years later when we were all at Ammah's house and Willie and I had been put to bed, my mother and grandmother stole quietly into my room for some reason. Thinking me asleep, they continued talking over a problem that concerned money. I was not asleep and could not help hearing.

My small mind jumped to the conclusion that my family needed money and that I must raise the needed amount. Now, we had with us two fisher-folk dolls, a man and a woman, evidently sent from France, with little gilt earrings in their ears that I was certain were solid gold and worth a great deal. I would take them to a pawnshop, I decided. (Mother had never mentioned the word "pawnshop" to us. I must have read it in some book.)

As soon as I could see my friend Ellinor Hays the next day, I confided my plans to her. Her common sense prevailed.

"There is no pawnshop in Carlisle, Laura," she said firmly.

"Then I'll take the earrings to Harrisburg."

"But you would need to pay for your fare on the train. You'd have to ask your mother for the money."

Grandmother Mary Lee Rose—Ammah—with William and Laura

"Well, wouldn't Robert do it for me?" Robert was Mr. Hays' factotum and handyman. He was constantly employed in various ways, among them, driving the horses.

"Oh, no! Robert would have to tell Papa, and Papa wouldn't like it and it would get us both into trouble."

I saw my benevolence melting into thin air. I don't recall ever telling my mother of this plan. It was years before I found out that the "problem" was a wayward son of Ammah, a wanderer who needed help continually, and that the earrings were only tin covered with gilt!

CHAPTER THREE

Sorrento

GRANDMOTHER Benét, who suffered from hayfever, found that she was free of her allergy in the wonderful air of the Maine coast, where many Army and Navy friends vacationed. So she bought a house at Sorrento, on a bluff looking directly over Frenchman's Bay toward Bar Harbor. Her cottage, which boasted a tower with stained-glass windows, was charmingly furnished in light rattan, and the dining-room china was Spode. There were two parlors, one with a fireplace; and upstairs there were three good-sized bedrooms, besides Grandmama's little studio where she painted.

The yearly trip to Maine to spend our vacation was always such fun. The visit began just when the city became most stuffy and the weather very hot. Trunks were packed and sent ahead of time. When the long-awaited day arrived, a well-filled lunch basket was a part of our luggage and of great interest to us. Father went with us to the station to put us on the Boston train. He usually joined us much later in the summer when he took his leave.

On one fateful occasion he did not watch the time carefully and we missed our train! Back we had to go, all the way home, and as we stumped along sleepily, I heard Willie crying softly at my side. Between sobs, he said, "Mother promised I was to have something out of the lunch basket as soon as we got on the train."

The maids luckily hadn't taken the sheets off our beds yet, and we passed another night at home. By the next day, our rolls were all eaten up, so Father had to go for a new supply for our lunch basket.

That lunch basket served us well, and after a supper from it that night, Willie and I were tucked into our lower berths. I remember well those trips to Maine and the ecstatic moment of each when the cooler air of Massachusetts began to be felt. Peeping under the window blind, I watched the houses in the towns we passed slip by and wondered what the people were like who lived in them. The lower berth was a joy to me and I made up stories about the people I would never know until I fell asleep.

Our second maid, named Mary, went with us one summer and had the upper berth over mine. She helped us to dress in the morning, for we were already in Boston when we woke. We got a cab and went to the Parker House for a good breakfast, and then Mother left us and the luggage in Mary's care while she went shopping for our serge suits—dark blue for every day and white for Sunday—and big straw hats. As we were so close in age, Willie and I were sometimes taken for twins.

When Mother came back, we had our usual Boston treat—a ride in the swan boats on the lake in the park. After an early supper at the Parker House, we boarded the Fall River boat where we spent the night. I don't know whether it was Mary or a nurse of a later summer who fell out of the upper berth on top of me, which was a shock. Luckily, no one was hurt.

After stopping at Bar Harbor, the Fall River boat took us to the wharf at Sorrento where Grandfather Benét—Grandpapa, we called him—met us and took us to Grandmama at the cottage.

I can best remember our Benét grandparents in this setting. Grandpapa, tall, benign, with his Catalonian ancestry showing in his splendid eyes and his courteous approach to everyone, was beloved by officials, assistants, friends, and neighbors. He had grown up in St. Augustine, Florida, the eldest son of the ten children of Pedro Benét of Minorca. Grandmama was charming and slight, and had the manners of a great lady. She was often engaged in copying in her tiny studio, and she allowed us to look at everything that she painted with such patient accuracy. I remember particularly a white dog. She, who could not originate, would have been blissfully happy had the Almighty bestowed upon her the genius of her two grandsons, whose success as poets she would not live to see.

At the end of our long trip began the happy summer days that were never long enough. There was no beach for us to play on, but there was the boardwalk fringed with rocks and berry bushes. Other children joined us and we played house in between the rocks, picked berries for meals, and made dishes out of leaves and stray shells, and necklaces out of pieces of seaweed. When the lunch hour came we went back to the cottage and, after lunch, took short naps which were soon given up.

Grandfather Stephen Vincent Benét

The afternoons were different. We could not wade or bathe in the icy Maine waters—anyone who did came out purple and shaking—but we could fish off the wharf, though we never caught anything interesting, only sculpins. Sometimes we played Witch-in-the-Wood with Willie's friends, the Davenport boys, and one day there was a candy pull. But when the molasses boiled, instead of pulling it, they smeared it over popcorn balls, which was a great disappointment to me.

Every day was an adventure. Sometimes we were taken for rides in marvelous carriages called buckboards, pulled by swift-running horses. There was no Indian colony in Sorrento but a few Indian women camped each year at the foot of the bluff on which Grandmama's cottage stood. They had delightful baskets woven of fragrant, different-colored grasses to sell, and Mother would always buy some.

When Sunday came, Mary (or another maid) forsook us for early Mass but soon returned. The rector of our Episcopal church, the Reverend Mr. J. S. Moody, had a children's service in the afternoon. The white church stood right in the center of a blueberry patch and the children invariably stopped to snatch a few of the ripest berries. During our last summer in Maine, Brewster Davenport and Willie were the ushers and passed the collection plates with great dignity.

I must mention the Ingersoll children. Mary had met their nurse at church, and so we became acquainted. There were two little girls, named Elaine and Enid. Elaine had brown eyes and brown curls. Enid, the younger, was a blonde and I remember Willie's chasing her around a bush and trying to kiss her. We only saw the girls occasionally, but I was obsessed with admiration for both of them and prayed every night fervently that we would see them again each summer. But we never did. When they left Sorrento that fall, they left permanently. They must have satisfied something intensely romantic in my nature. To this day I remember just how they looked and how they dressed.

On nights of storm, the wind howled across Frenchman's Bay from Bar Harbor, from which the grownups brought

Laura and William photographed by Uncle Larry during one of the later summers at Sorrento

Japanese dolls when they went shopping there. Willie and I shared a bedroom right beside the tower with the stained-glass windows. When the wind blew briskly around it, and I was safe in bed, I thought of the verse from Edmund Lear's *Nonsense Book* about the Jumblies who, on a stormy day, on a winter's morn, sailed off to sea in a sieve:

> *"Far and few, far and few*
> *Are the lands where the Jumblies live;*
> *Their heads are green, and their hands are blue,*
> *And they went to sea in a sieve."*

I'd repeat it to myself, while worrying about the poor Jumblies, traveling to their distant lands in such a flimsy boat.

Before the summer ended, Father usually came, and one year Uncle Larry appeared and took a picture of us. Uncle Larry was always lots of fun. Beloved Sorrento, how many happy times we all spent in that cottage Grandmama named "By-the-Sea."

CHAPTER FOUR

Frankford Arsenal

WHEN I recollect Frankford Arsenal, my thoughts are happy ones. I remember our arrival at this post in the town of Bridesburg near Philadelphia. We went there from Washington when I was about six. I was holding tightly to my father's hand as we went up the path to our new quarters.

The Arsenal itself was built in a sort of quadrangle. On the right side of the entrance was the commanding officer's set of quarters, roomy and stately, as it was the largest and the best. The office lay beyond it. To the left was our set of quarters in a double house, and beyond, a single house that we later learned was occupied by a family named Baker. Then the post stretched off into shops, and the lodgings and barracks of both single and married soldiers.

This post had a country-like appearance. The lawns were

grassy and spacious. There were haycocks on them in summer when the grass was cut. There were vegetable and flower gardens for the use of the officers' families. Only the commanding officer had a greenhouse. A kindly gardener who brought Mother fresh flowers in season remarked on his first visit, "Twice a week, Ma'am, I'll have them for ye, and when ye have company."

Our house proved to be very pleasant, with a large living room, dining room, pantry, laundry, and kitchen in succession. Upstairs in the front were two good-sized bedrooms (Willie and I shared a room there), and a back hall led to a guest room and our playroom—ours exclusively. At one end my dolls, with their own furniture, took up their abode. Midway in the room stood the dollhouse. The other end was Willie's and possessed shelves which held our books and his drawings and coloring pencils and blunt scissors.

From his earliest days when he could barely hold a pencil, Willie's delight was in trying to draw and paint animals. What he accomplished did not please him and he resolved to write to Uncle Larry in Paris. His request was brief:

Dear Uncle Larry;
   Will you please draw me a lion and lioness with cubs?
                              Your loving nephew,
                                    Willie

Alas, when the reply came, Uncle Larry plainly showed that he was quite as unable to conceive lions as his nephew was. He did, however, draw a sizable hen and close beside her a huge egg as large as she was. Underneath was the letter, prized for many years:

Dear William:
   I wanted to draw with a pen
   A lion and cubs in a den.
   When the lion I saw and heard his loud roar,
   I decided to draw you a hen.
                        Love from your Uncle Larry

As a script surrounding the hen was written: "Don't you think this is a nice hen and don't you think she has laid a big egg?"

We made our first young friend at Frankford soon after our arrival. Adelaide Mitcham was several years our senior but she was full of kindness toward us. She must have noticed that we were lonesome and shy, with nothing to do, and said invitingly, "Don't you want to come over to our house and see our frogs? We have lots of them—tadpoles turning into frogs."

We were ushered into the other half of the double set of quarters. Sure enough, there were the laundry tubs all full of polliwogs which were changing piecemeal into frogs, one leg at a time. We lingered, fascinated and happy.

But several months later, Mother told us that Mrs. Mitcham was taking her family to Europe. We missed Adelaide and her younger sister, the naturalist who raised the frogs, even though we looked forward with curiosity to the arrival of new neighbors.

Much as we loved frogs and all living creatures, for a while our only live pets except for an occasional kitten were the bantam chickens Father bought and named for the Queen of the Nile and two famous Romans—Cleopatra, Mark Antony, and Julius Caesar. Later on, a gentle bantam hen named plain Annie was added to the collection, and my brother once whispered to me, "Lollie, Cleopatra has disturbed Annie off her nest and she is swelling with rage." There was spirit in Annie even if she had no title.

In the early days at Frankford when Mother had gone to Philadelphia for the day, Willie and I washed a yellow kitten in the bathroom and got hairs all over everything. Then we took the kitten into the guest room to dry it. When Mother got home she wrapped the kitten in a towel and scolded us for our cruelty to it.

She also was indignant about the guest room. Her sister was expected that night, and Mother looked at the pillow, covered with yellow fur. "There, now," she said. "Auntie has to lay her head there tonight, and it is all over hairs."

"Well, the kitten needed it," we defended ourselves.

"Oh, no," replied Mother firmly. "Cats don't like water." She was hardly ever annoyed at us, though she was that day. In fact, her family often spoke of "Fan's fearful indulgence of those children."

For a short time, we did have a dog—the excellent Jolly, who appeared one day on our doormat and adopted us. His breed was nonexistent; his coat was a nondescript black and white; but he had a fine head and an amiable disposition— and he was Willie's delight. For reasons unknown to us, Father dubbed him the "Siberian Bloodhound" in letters to his parents.

One day, Grandfather Benét paid us a visit. Grandmama did not come with him but sent me a miniature yellow bonnet filled with candy. Willie received a ball—"With which," said Grandpapa, as he handed it to him, "you are to kill the Siberian Bloodhound."

Alas, poor Jolly's stay with us was not a long one. Mrs. Pitman, who had moved with her husband into the Mitcham's vacant quarters next door, had a small lap dog called Gyppie. Her husband told Father that Mrs. Pitman was afraid some harm might come to Gyppie from the larger dog. Father always dreaded bickering and unpleasantness so he said he would give the dog away. He found Jolly a home outside the gates of the Arsenal, and poor Willie's distress at the loss of his comrade was pathetic. "I shall have five dogs when I grow up," he said to console himself.

In spite of this, I was a favorite of Mrs. Pitman, who often took me driving with her. While she sat in the back with Gyppie, I sat on the front seat with the driver where I could look out over the horses' ears and see everything. How I loved it! No matter how far we rode, it was never far enough to satisfy me. For some reason, Mrs. Pitman never invited Willie to ride with us.

Surrounded as we were by adults, we pined for companions of our own age. Of course, Captain Baker's family had a whole house to live in right next door (he ranked Father), but we considered his children to be babies. The elder, Harris, was not yet five but he did eventually come to play with us one never-to-be-forgotten day!

As soon as we had settled into our new home, Mother, who was a natural teacher and had, indeed, been one before her marriage, began our lessons. Each day, the green cloth that covered the dining room table was folded up and the lesson books laid out. Willie could not read yet, so Father volunteered to take him on as a pupil. Education begins at home, and ours certainly did.

In the evening after our early supper, two rattan stools were brought out and placed by Mother's chair, and she would read aloud to us until bedtime from *St. Nicholas*, Dickens,

James Walker Benét—Father

Scott, and eventually Thackeray. This story hour, the best time of the day, came just after Willie had his reading lesson with Father, who taught him in a most peculiar manner. "Take the word 'Mother,'" said Father. "M-o-t, mot; h-e-r, her; Mot-her."

Frances Rose Benét—Mother

I cannot recall what other words poor Willie struggled with, but the lesson was soon over.

Always, as soon as our daytime lessons were done, Mother sent us out to play, unless the weather was bad. Quite often we acted out a story that Mother had read to us the night before. When the tale of Robin Hood had been read, Willie and I exchanged "buffets," he as Robin Hood and I as Little John. But a sad disappointment was in store for me when we tried to impersonate the characters from one of Grimm's fairy tales, in which the brother of the youthful heroine was changed into a fawn. In the tale, the loving sister took off her little golden garter and fastened it around the soft neck of the fawn, so that she might always recognize him. But when I tried to unpin my garter, which was anything but golden, I could not get it loose from my Ferris waist, which was part of the underclothing that little girls wore then. So that game had to be given up.

Little Harris Baker's momentous visit followed the introduction of a new game that soon became our favorite. Why we were so enamoured of it I cannot tell. Mother had given me Charles Dickens' *Child's History of England* to read aloud during my lessons, and a gruesome book it was. It must have been from there that the game "Bloody Mary" swam into our ken. When we played this game—and this without Mother's knowledge—two chairs were drawn together to make a bier. The green cloth was stolen from the dining room table to cover them. Candles in their silver candlesticks were lighted and placed near. I was Bloody Mary, installed on the bier, and Willie's rôle was that of her attendant priest.

I had learned the Queen's dying speech and said in sepulchral tones: "When I am dead and my body is opened, ye shall find the word 'Calais' written on my heart." I then sighed and closed my eyes and Willie announced solemnly, "Queen Mary is dead."

We thoroughly enjoyed the whole proceeding and played

it often. Of course, the candlesticks and the cloth were carefully put back when we had finished.

So when little Harris came over to play, we thought nothing could be more entertaining for him than the game of Bloody Mary. When he in a fright began to cry and rushed home, we were delighted, for we had thought him a terrible baby and a drag on our game. But next day there was a reckoning. When Father came home from the office to lunch, he said sternly, "What did you children play yesterday that frightened Harris? He had terrible nightmares and his parents were up with him all night."

We shamefacedly explained about Bloody Mary. I think that Father was secretly amused, for he did not punish us, merely said gravely, "Harris is younger than you and more easily frightened. You should never have played a game like that with him. Play something pleasant next time."

We never had the opportunity. The redoubtable Harris was never left in our charge again. His family knew better.

Mother was not only our teacher but she was our church and Sunday school as well. Because the town of Bridesburg was apt to be full of sickness and was also quite dirty, I cannot remember either parent going there to church, nor did we ever go there to school. But every Sunday morning we were at Mother's knee while she showed us colored cards of the Old Testament stories that she read aloud in her lovely voice. The Epistle and Gospel were also read from our Episcopal prayer book. We learned by heart the Collect for each Sunday. Our dear mother said there was no more interesting book than the Bible and she made it fascinating for us.

Mother had many relatives and friends in and around Philadelphia. As all of them wanted to see the Arsenal and as all were fond of Mother, we had frequent visitors—some of them old ladies—and they all brought us gifts.

I remember Aunt Annie Sutton with pleasure. She had been the head of the school from which Mother was graduated. She wore a small lace cap and brought us a book of the kings and queens of England. Pointing to Edward VI, she said in tones so sympathetic that he might have been her dead son, "That poor young man died of consumption." She liked children and understood them.

There were Mother's three maiden aunts from Philadelphia—Aunt Sophie, Aunt Gertrude, and Aunt Kate Neill—who always dressed in black. One of them said once, with a twinkle in her eye, "Speak to your *black* aunts, Willie."

Then there was Great-aunt Agnes Mahon—Aunt Aggie—an excellent person who liked practical jokes, as well as riddles that we never understood. Now it happened that I had been enjoying the story—an English fairy tale—of Mr. and Mrs. Vinegar who lived snugly with furniture and a canary in a vinegar bottle. So when Aunt Aggie said to me, "Laura, would you like to walk *into* a bottle?" I was entranced and said, "Yes," thinking of entering a bottle with a small doll family living inside it.

"Then go and ask the cook for an empty bottle."

When I returned with a large one, Aunt Aggie had me place it right across the sill of the door leading into the room where we were sitting. "Now shut your eyes and get down on your hands and knees and crawl toward the bottle."

This I did, planning all the time how I would place my furniture. I knew it was a fairy tale, but fairy tales came true, didn't they? I bumped into something. Then Aunt Aggie's voice broke the silence.

Great-aunt Agnes Mahon—Aunt Aggie—in her later years

"Now you can open your eyes! See, you've walked into a bottle."

I did as she bid, and oh, what a shocking disappointment! There, where I had knocked against it, lay the empty vinegar bottle with no little home in it, no canary, no table or chairs. I began to cry bitterly. I had trusted grown-up people but I never trusted them again. I ran from the room, sobbing, Mother calling after me, "Why, dear, it was just a little joke." Little joke, indeed! It was a heartbreak. Aunt Aggie was a breaker-up of homes, I thought.

This episode made a dent on my memory that I never forgot. Other visitors never did things of this kind. Father secretly made up a rhyme about Aunt Aggie and another relative we called Aunt Ditty, who came with her for a visit. It was addressed to Willie:

> He thought he saw the family cat
> Who'd found a little kitty,
> He looked again and found it was
> Aunt Aggie and Aunt Ditty.
> "I am so diffident," he said,
> "They look at me with pity."

Though Mother was our main source of entertainment and gaiety, Father had certain accomplishments and talents that belonged to him alone. One was the fashioning of tiny pigs out of lemons. Four matches made the pig's legs, and his snout and ears were easily done by cutting the rind of the lemon with a penknife. Sun umbrellas for the pigs were geranium leaves. And then, with our pigs, we mounted a high board fence that we called Jumbo and chanted:

> "Oh, here we are on Jumbo,
> Below the lovely sun,
> And Piggy with his sun umbrella
> Is here to join in the fun!"

Another piece of property that gave untold pleasure was a decrepit wheelbarrow with one side out. We adored it, but why I don't know. When we were told a little friend was coming to visit us, we agreed to lend it to her, as a great privilege.

And now to return to Father. Mother seldom left us for a

whole day. But occasionally she did take a day off to do some shopping in Philadelphia, an hour away.

When Father returned from the office and dark fell suddenly and dinner time was approaching, Willie and I felt pretty solemn and began to watch the gate from the upstairs windows of Mother's bedroom. In deep tones, Father would say to the clock on Mother's mantle, "Strike the last hour!" and the clock would obey him instantly—how, we never knew. But though the clock impressively struck the last hour, Mother did not return. Then Father would remark in a dreamy voice, "I really think your mother has followed a wagon out of town."

This was a terrible thought. How could our pretty young mother, who dressed so becomingly, get interested in following some old wagon? Perhaps she would stop at some strange town and never come back to us. Oh, woe, woe! Tears came to my eyes when I thought of it. And just then we heard the familiar sound of the front door opening, and Mother's voice!

I remember one adventure when I was seven that might have resulted in tragedy. Frankford Arsenal stood on the bank of the Delaware River and at the rear of the grounds was a boathouse from which officers could take out rowboats. One bright afternoon in spring Father proposed taking Mother for a row on the river. Mother was delighted and took me with her, leaving Willie at home with our two Irish maids. Both parents were good oarsmen. But unfortunately, when we had gone some distance down the river, a strong wind began to blow and the current set dead against us.

They rowed, rowed hard and desperately, but could make no headway back toward the boathouse. Wrapped in my mother's jacket, I whimpered softly in the bow, terrified by the black water, the wind, and my parents' blistered hands which had already begun to bleed. They had to tie handkerchiefs over their palms to keep any purchase on their oars. Many a boat passed us and was hailed, and help asked in urgent tones, but the owners paid no attention. It seemed literally impossible to get past a certain spot on the river bank. We should certainly have capsized (and none of us could swim) but the wind lulled suddenly. Father landed us at long last and my mother dragged me up the bank. I fell on the warm earth, fairly clawing it in the pure relief of being on land again. When at last we reached the house, Willie and the maids were lifting up their voices together in fright and sorrow, thinking us drowned. Word had drifted in to them of our whereabouts.

Our long wait for comrades of our own age was at last ended. The Clarks, our former neighbors in Springfield Arsenal, had been ordered to Frankford! When they arrived, to our surprise and delight, they took the set of quarters next to us which had been vacated by the Pitmans.

Helen Clark had blue eyes, and her long dark ringlets were my envy, my hair being straight as a string. Miriam Clark, my best friend at Frankford Arsenal, was not as handsome as Helen but she had far more originality. She was my height, had brown hair which she wore loose, brown eyes, and a delightful disposition.

Happy times began for all of us! Helen Clark, who was two years older than Miriam, and Willie were the two most thrillingly involved in the plays and acting, the costumes and scenery that began to fill our days at Frankford. They, in company with the Clarks' visiting cousin, Maxwell Murray, organized a theater in one of the vacant rooms on the ground floor of the Clark quarters. Because the furniture had not yet arrived from their last post in the West, we were in full possession of the big empty rooms. Miriam Clark and myself with our various dolls constituted a suitable audience. Neither one of us pined to act, but we looked on, listened, clapped enthusiastically, and enjoyed ourselves immensely.

There was one really miraculous camel composed of the two boys and tall, handsome Helen, the only one fit to be the hump in the middle. The camel staggered at least halfway across the stage before it disintegrated. After the camel episode, the actors did a scene out of *Uncle Tom's Cabin*—Eliza crossing the icy river when freedom beckoned from the other side. Her feet were supposed to be cut and bleeding, and Willie said proudly, "We had a real red cloth for blood."

Then Miriam suggested that an exciting drama could be made out of Scott's *The Lady of the Lake*. This idea was seized upon at once, for a prisoner was to be walled up alive, with meager refreshments placed beside him to comfort his last hours. Each actor wished to take the part of the prisoner, especially when the "roots and water and bread" of the poem turned out to be ginger ale and jelly cake, or homemade wine and gingerbread. Then the prisoner would stick his head out from between the chairs that walled him in and say in a squeaky voice, "My roots and water and bread is good!" A mutiny followed as we all argued to take the place of the prisoner.

Miriam had a remarkable doll named Navarre Christine, which many years later was presented to a museum. Once when Miriam and I were sitting on the floor playing paper dolls, she glanced up and screamed, "He's whipping Navarre." We rushed to the other side of the room, where her cousin Maxwell was indeed whipping the doll. Maxwell was what was then known as a "limb." At another time, he hung Harry and Gretchen, two other beloved dolls, upside down on the clothesline.

It must have been when the Clarks were with us that we instituted the game of "Long Hide-and-Seek." There were all manner of satisfactory hiding places around the shops and warehouses (Frankford was a manufacturing Arsenal) known only to us. Oh, that free, frantic chase over lawns and fields to achieve a good burrowing place before the hunt fairly started, its members whooping and hallooing like Indians!

On days of high wind when we were alone, Willie and I played a game we had invented called "Catching Hurricanes." Starting from a hillock, we ran with the wind, drawing in long breaths of it, propelled and carried by it till we paused some distance away. This game gave us a sense of great exaltation.

Meanwhile, our generous Grandmother Benét was planning a special surprise for Christmas. The gift was kept a profound secret. Our parlor had long French windows and the day after Christmas when Willie and I were idly looking out, a pony and cart driven by a soldier dashed up and stopped at the door. We were ecstatic when we found out the pony was for us. His name was General Grant, and he was a Shetland, in part at least, with a long mane and tail.

But we did not have a chance to enjoy that pony to the full until some time later. Almost at once orders came to return to Washington, and we had to pack up and leave our new treasure to be driven about and petted by the Clarks.

CHAPTER FIVE

Bethlehem

AFTER a short stay in Washington, where we lived again at our grandparents' home at 1717 I Street, our next move was to Bethlehem, Pennsylvania, where Father's duty would be with the Bethlehem Iron Company. While there, he would not have to wear a uniform.

He went on ahead and worked hard trying to secure a suitable house for us to live in. One day, Mother received a letter containing this rhyme:

> J.B. Zimmerle, he
> Says he *will* rent to Captain B—

and a roomy house with a large yard full of fruit trees was ours for fifty dollars a month in the fall of 1895.

It must have been September when we, with the pony and cart, the dollhouse, and all our prized possessions, arrived at

But after a few minutes he would forget his promise and travel along as fast as ever.

family worth knowing. The bantam chickens did not move with us; they were probably sold.

We were not long in discovering that Bethlehem was an old, charming, and interesting town. It had been settled, with nearby Nazareth, by the Moravians, a close-knit and kindly folk of German extraction who called themselves the United Brethren. Across the river was South Bethlehem, in which Lehigh College was located, as well as the suburb of Fountain Hill, the section where the élite and wealthy, including a few Moravians, resided.

During the fine, brisk autumn days of our first fall in Bethlehem, Father sometimes took us for walks outside the town on Sunday afternoons. Mother would say, as we started out, "Remember, Jack, their legs are short and yours are long, and you forget and walk too fast. Then they get overheated and catch cold."

Father would begin to chant, as we walked along:

>"Nice slow walk,
>Do not fret or talk,
>Mother will scold,
>If you take cold.
>Nice-slow-walk."

348 Market Street. When the neighboring children caught sight of General Grant and the pony cart, they decided we were a

The walk I remember most vividly is one to Rittersville, a little village about a mile or so from Bethlehem. To reach it, we crossed a bridge over a canal. In the middle of the bridge there was a blood-red sign—BREAD—in large letters. That was enough for Father. He began a tale at once.

"Yes, it was too sad. The poor girl was engaged to the baker's son, fell off the bridge into the canal, and was drowned before they could rescue her. Her heartbroken lover cried:

> " 'The waters closed about her head,
> Rittersville, oh, Rittersville.'
> With bloody fingers he wrote 'BREAD'
> On the bonny canal at Rittersville."

The sluggish canal did not look to us as if it could drown anybody, but we were delighted with this saga, even though we did not always strictly believe Father's stories. Another one he told us was about a green house we saw on one of our walks.

"In that house," he said, "lives a cross-eyed daughter with an agèd father. They subsist entirely on stale bread and peanuts. And they keep a parrot that sings out all day, 'You're another.' "

I think it is a shame that Father did not write fiction.

Over the years in Bethlehem I went to several birthday parties. I remember one that I attended when we first moved there; I did not know any of the other children. The party was in charge of a bustling female relative. There was a game that tested our memories. On the lawn was a large table covered with objects of many kinds—camera, vase, pocketbook, eyeglasses, et cetera. Every child was given paper and pencil, and after a few minutes of time to study the table, the objects on it were hidden from our view.

A prize was to be given to the boy or girl who could make the longest list of the things we had seen. I had already inspected the prizes and had seen a sheet of paper dolls that I coveted.

But my paper had only about six objects on it when the relative announced, "Time's up. Hand in your lists."

After a few minutes of checking, she said, "Deborah Smith wins with twenty objects named," and she handed out the first prize.

Then, "Laura Benét receives the booby prize," and, oh, bliss, she handed me the whole sheet of paper dolls! I was so happy to have them I did not mind at all being the booby.

We as a family had barely arrived in Bethlehem when the question of schools came up. Neither Willie nor I had ever been to school, but Mother by this time had taught us all the rudiments, including the multiplication tables.

A woman named Ida MacMullen was running a first-rate kindergarten on our very own Market Street. Although Willie was above the average age, he used his hands so deftly that our parents decided to enroll him there. Later on he would be able to have the advantage of an older-level afternoon class that Miss MacMullen conducted. I mourned exceedingly that I could not go to the kindergarten with him, so fascinating was it in all its aspects. But I was ten, and too old.

Willie adjusted immediately to his new school and fashioned clay flower pots and tiny Washington monuments with those clever fingers of his—the longest fingers, in his maturity, that I have ever seen. He was most happy walking to school each morning, carrying his lunch in a bag, and he was liked by every child there. I visited the kindergarten a few times, a rare privilege.

Sarah Myers was Willie's favorite among the girls. After a minor accident at school, Father made up a verse about her, supposedly written by Willie:

> My admiration never tires
> For the lovely Sarah Myers.
> When her nose began to bleed,
> I felt very sad indeed.

Trombone belfry of the Moravian Church, Bethlehem, Pennsylvania

The Moravian Seminary (hours nine to twelve, and two to four) was a fine old-fashioned school with both boarding and day pupils. Some of the boarders were the children of missionaries stationed in foreign lands. This is where I began my formal education. I soon discovered that the Moravian Seminary building had been a hospital at the time of the American Revolution. At its corner stood the noble old church, with a belfry whose trombones were played on special occasions, most frequently for deaths. Father told Willie and me that when the trumpet-like brasses played fast, the victim had died of a galloping consumption; when they played slowly, the illness of the deceased had been a long decline.

Down the street from the Seminary were the Sisters' charming house, the Brethren's house, and the widows' house. I soon learned to shorten my trip to school by walking through the cemetery where the stones were flat and the men and women were separated.

At that time, Dr. Hark was the principal, and we walked two-and-two into chapel every morning under his watchful eye. He always wore a long black gown. The Moravian catechism was very like that of the Episcopal Church and not hard for me to memorize.

I was very shy at first in the long corridors and unfamiliar rooms. I soon found that all the pupils were divided into what were called "Room Companies" with a teacher presiding over each group. Our guardian was Mrs. Fitzpatrick, who taught plain sewing and looked like a benevolent owl. She also supervised the younger girls. I was very fond of her but very poor at sewing. My "patch," as it was called, was always grimy.

In the yard of the Seminary were great wooden swings that we enjoyed at recess. We used to play what was known as a "twist up" and a "run under." In the latter, the swinger was sent up so high that it was terrifying.

One day when I was still new at the Seminary I was swinging with a girl I did not know when she suddenly said, "I want a blackie. I'm hungry."

"What's a blackie?" I wanted to know.

"You'll see. Come with me."

Taking me by the hand, she dashed across the street to a small frame building connected with the Sisters' house. We climbed three or four steps and there, outside the door, on a piece of clean paper, lay a pile of tiny crisp molasses pies, each about the size of a small butter plate. They cost only a few cents apiece, so we left the money and flew back to school, because recess was almost over. But there was still time to munch rapturously on our molasses treats. The Sisters were noted far and wide for these delicious Moravian delicacies and especially for their peppermints.

Miss Lang, who taught arithmetic and music, was a thorn in my flesh. I knew only elementary arithmetic—to add, subtract, multiply, and divide. She used to give us "solutions," which I never could solve. Another girl in my class, Mary Grider, could solve them with ease, and my soul was filled with envy and dread.

But on at least one occasion I was able to please the terrifying Miss Lang, whose name was always pronounced "Long." She wanted a bow and arrow, and I volunteered the information that my brother had one. When I arrived at school with the article that Willie had lent, I also carried a note from him, explaining:

> Dear Miss Long,
> That arrow won't shoot strait.

I think Miss Lang had a better opinion of me from that time on.

One afternoon when he grew a little older, Willie drove to my school with General Grant and the cart, and was lured into the Seminary grounds where Dr. Hark's two little girls, Hilda and Anna, begged for a ride. Willie let them climb into the cart, but unfortunately, in the big yard, there was a hillock. The pony stumbled and the cart lurched to one side. Both children fell out. Luckily they were not hurt, but they were terrified lest their father find out they had not asked permission and punish them. I don't think he ever found out. Tenderhearted Willie must have thought their father a monster, as we were never whipped, not even when he went out driving with some of the boys and ran over a farmer's turkey.

Willie got into several scrapes during the years we were in Bethlehem. His companions when out of school were the boys in the block, since they were about his age. Fred Conlin, who lived directly across the street, was the leader of the group. Willie was far more innocent than the rest, and one day when they were all teasing the Conlin's cook and shouting, "Oh, look at her, she's lousy," he echoed the word, not knowing what it meant. He was a frank child and told Mother about it later.

She was horrified. "Do you know, dear, what that word means?"

"No, I don't," replied Willie.

"It means 'covered with vermin.' To think of describing a poor, hard-working cook in such language! After dinner we will go over, you and I, and you must apologize to her."

Go they did. I watched, awe stricken, at the window, as Mother and Willie crossed the street and went to the Conlin's back door! The apology was given, the cook was overwhelmed, and the peacemakers returned home. That little episode was highly characteristic of Mother. She hated injustice of any kind.

It may have been that same winter that the Ben Burger episode took place. On our side of Market Street at the corner lived a prosperous German bachelor of that name. His housekeeper took beautiful care of him and, on one particular afternoon after a heavy snowfall, she had brushed the front steps clean. The crowd of some half-dozen boys loved to tease her, she was so prim and old-maidish. First they threw snow over the steps, and then, during a fresh onslaught, a hard snowball

Laura and William

broke a pane of glass in one of the shining windows. Hearing the enraged housekeeper coming to the door, the boys tore off in every direction, leaving Willie standing there, somewhat dazed.

The old dame vented her fury on him. "You'll go to jail for this! Mr. Burger will come over tonight and see Captain Benét."

How well I remember that awful afternoon! I did not get out of school until four o'clock, and it was nearly dark by then. My bag of books was heavy as I trudged along through the cold. I was almost home when a neighboring girl, Isabel Higgins, ran toward me through the snow. "Oh, oh," she called out, "have you heard? Your brother Willie has got himself into a nice scrape."

"What's the matter?" I asked anxiously.

So Isabel told me the whole story. The world whirled around before my eyes. Willie in jail! I didn't stop to listen to any more chatter. When I got into the house I found that Father and Mother were both out, and Willie was in the sitting room, shivering and frightened to death, seeing himself already behind bars.

By the time Mother and Father came in, dinner was already late and there was no time to confess. The soup had been served when the doorbell rang. We saw a man being ushered into the parlor, and the maid returned to say that Mr. Burger would like to see Captain Benét.

Father rose at once. Mr. Burger had a deep voice and we heard snatches of their conversation. But Father was equal to him.

"I don't want to chastise the lad," said Mr. Burger thickly.

"It won't be necessary," said Father, "I can attend to my son. I shall stop his allowance until the pane of glass is paid for. Please tell me how much it will cost."

Mr. Burger, who seemed mollified, named the amount. It was paid at once, so he took his leave and Father returned to eat his dinner. He looked more amused than otherwise, but Mother was much distressed.

As for poor Willie, the vision of jail slowly faded and he began to relax. The punishment was only to lose his twenty-five cents a week. Father questioned him after dinner, realized that he had been made the scapegoat, and said, "You must never join in such a performance again, my son. It is wanton mischief, and keep away from that Conlin boy."

The bicycle was becoming very popular at this time, so Father bought one for the family. It was a cushioned-tired bicycle, which was less expensive than the more fashionable pneumatic-tired affairs.

Mother, who always wanted to do everything, bought herself a neat little outfit and resolved to learn to ride the bicycle. She began to take lessons from a teacher, but Willie and I learned quickly on our own and rode everywhere.

After Mother had taken quite a few lessons, Father inquired if she could ride alone.

"Oh, yes," said Mother, full of enthusiasm. "I can ride splendidly if the man who is teaching me keeps his hand on the back of the seat." Father did not reply, but he obviously had his doubts.

Alas, there came a day when there was no hand on the back of the seat, a day that might have ended in tragedy. It happened that Father, who played an excellent game of tennis, was enjoying a set with three other enthusiasts on a rented court halfway to Main Street on a sloping hill.

As they were changing partners, one man cried, "Why, Benét, there comes your wife down the hill at top speed. Quick, quick! The bicycle's run away with her."

The four men rushed out and formed a cordon across the street. It took their united efforts and all their strength to stop the runaway wheel and rescue Mother. That was the end of riding for her. She never mounted the bicycle again.

Willie had his own adventure with a bicycle some years later. A teacher named Vogel, although not especially popular with his scholars, invited Willie's whole class to a luncheon at the Sun Inn in South Bethlehem. They were to meet and bicycle across the river and up quite a steep hill to the hotel. They were all to decorate their bicycles for the ride.

It happened that Willie, more fortunate than most, had a

friend, Frank Betge, who was skilled in the art of decoration. Though not invited to the feast because he attended another school, Frank generously made Willie's bicycle a thing of beauty with colored paper.

It was a hot summer day when Willie started off triumphantly to join the other boys. We did not expect him back until late afternoon, of course. But when suppertime came and no William, we began to wonder what had happened to him. We were all seated on the front porch in the cool evening air when a familiar figure appeared in the distance, wheeling a bicycle.

My brother, who had left with the air of a conqueror, was trying to keep back the tears. The whole tragedy of the day was explained in a few simple words. His cushion-tired bicycle could not take the hill beyond which the Sun Inn lay. One by one his comrades passed him, for they all had pneumatic tires on their bicycles. One faithful friend waited for him as long as he could, and the two of them pushed and struggled to propel the wheel and make it go ahead. All their efforts were in vain. Willie was finally left alone at the foot of the hill. No lunch for him, and no festivities.

Mother spread a good supper for him on the dining room table, but before Willie touched it, he stripped his bicycle of its gay trimmings. That day of anguish was a turning point, for Father ordered a pneumatic-tired bicycle from Hartford at once.

As a small girl I was always interested in babies and thought large families wonderful. I bitterly regretted that there were only the two of us. One day on my way to school I passed down Church Street and saw a number of children, boys and girls, playing happily in their yard.

William, aged seven years

My friend, Mildred Myers, who was with me, answered my questions about them. "Those are the Williams children. There are seven of them—Olive, Cornelia, Bessie, Ned, Norman, Amory, and Wentworth. Their father's a professor at Lehigh."

"Don't they go to school?" I asked.

"No, I think they have a governess."

"Oh," I sighed, "then I can never meet them." It seemed the height of bliss to be one of seven.

However, one day I had a wonderful surprise. Olive, the eldest Williams girl, and her two sisters had all been entered at the Seminary and they were in my Room Company. I walked to chapel with Olive and that was the beginning of a true friendship that continued by letter even after we left Bethlehem. One of my greatest pleasures was to go to meals at the Williams house, and once I was invited there to a Valentine party.

"Cornelia Williams sews beautifully," Mrs. Fitzpatrick used to say. "Olive sews well, but not as well as Cornelia."

Then suddenly something happened that ended my days at the Seminary. One of the boarding pupils developed malignant diphtheria. Mother took me out at once, and though there were no other cases, I was never sent back to the Seminary. And I was very sorry.

Instead, Willie and I went to Miss MacMullen's afternoon classes for older children. We did not distinguish ourselves and must have sorely tried that good woman's patience. She gave us the poem *Evangeline*, Longfellow's sad story of evicted families and lovers parted for a lifetime, to study. My mind was not on Gabriel and Evangeline, however, but on the poor families, the children and parents often parted as they were cruelly made to leave home and possessions and board the ships. I was firmly convinced then that if our mother left the house she might never return. Mother finally wrote a note to Ida MacMullen asking her to select another poem for me as this one evidently made me nervous and reduced me to tears. Miss MacMullen was quite offended.

The next fall we were enrolled at the Moravian Parochial School and, to my joy, so were the Williams children. The skills of the Moravian Sisters included the making of beeswax candles. Each year when the Moravian Parochial School closed for the Christmas holiday, the boys and girls alternately sang Christmas hymns and hosannas in the old church. When at last the service was finished and the great doors were opened, a sister stood there holding a tray of small, lighted beeswax candles for the students. The legend was that if you could reach home with your candle still alight, you would have good fortune in the new year.

Another charming custom was the *putz*, as much a part of old Bethlehem as the trombones in the church belfry. The *putz* or Nativity scene was arranged in the front window of a house, in the homes of both the poor and the well-to-do. Viewers went to the front door, asked to see the *putz*, and looked in the window. In the poor homes, a donation of some coins was generally made. Of course the well-to-do homes had the more elegant displays.

It was while we were living in Bethlehem that we suffered a double loss. One late January day when the snow had begun to fly, Father and Mother were telegraphed for, as Grandfather Benét was dying in Washington. They had to hurry off with no farewells for Willie and me, but a neighbor came to share our loneliness until Ammah, who had been summoned from Carlisle, could reach us. She stayed with us for several weeks. Our grandfather's death was a great sorrow to us, for Willie and I were devoted to him.

That was the end of the house at 1717 I Street, as Grandmother Benét could not live there alone. Uncle Larry urged her to come to Paris and live with him. He offered to find a suitable apartment, a maid and a cook, which he did. And so our beloved grandmother sailed off across the ocean to spend the rest of her life in France.

CHAPTER SIX

Enter Stephen

As the years passed by in Bethlehem, it seemed an increasing problem to get a cook. While I was still at the Moravian Seminary we were taking our meals at Mrs. Schwartz' boardinghouse part of the time. Finally, our parents decided to move to the Eagle Hotel. They were expecting new orders soon, so they gave up the house on Market Street and engaged three rooms and a sitting room at the Eagle. The hotel was on Main Street, opposite the Moravian Parochial School, which by that time we were both attending.

At first we enjoyed ordering meals, but that pleasure palled, especially as Marcellus, our waiter, dallied over our breakfast so that we were nearly always late for the morning session of school.

The nicest boys on Fountain Hill rode over on their bicycles to the Moravian school—Will Estes, Jim Jenkins, Bill Duncan.

Willie became friends with all of them. Will Estes was a natural student and the best of them all, receiving the highest marks and prizes. He was the doctor's son.

Dancing school also entered our lives about this time, one of the great pleasures of my teen-age life. Norman Merriman and the Sayre brothers, Nevin and Frank, usually singled me out. Nevin glided gracefully, but Frank, who had red hair, usually stepped on my feet. We did the Lancers which was difficult, the waltz which was my favorite, the two step, and the Virginia reel.

At first, Jim Jenkins' sister, Marian, taught the class. But she soon gave it up and someone else who was a far better teacher took her place. Olive and Cornelia Williams both joined the class, and all the Fountain Hill girls.

Later, Mrs. Estes, the doctor's wife, organized a singing class in her apartment. It was conducted by Dr. Fred Wolle, a grand musician who was later the originator of the Bach Festival. He proved to be my friend. It seemed that Frank Sayre had sent me a Valentine, and this aroused great jealousy in the breasts of the Fountain Hill belles. A row of chairs was placed for the pupils, and the other girls determined to push back my chair so that I should sit on the floor. But their revenge was never accomplished because they could only manage to do it while we were singing in chorus. And Professor Wolle did not ask us to sing in chorus on that particular day. He may have had an inkling of what was going to happen. I, the innocent victim, knew nothing of all this until much later when Jean Estes told me. We were friendly at one time and exchanged many confidences.

But either that winter or the next, an epidemic of measles started in Bethlehem and attacked poor Willie. I remember a party to which we were invited while Willie was still sick and could not go. On this occasion he had planned to wear his new tuxedo, which I called his "tuck-seated." I had to go alone and was left sitting on the sofa while the others paired off and whispered about me, a stranger to them. I didn't enjoy that party. My turn with the measles followed Willie's.

After the measles came the whooping cough. Our friend Percy Werlich came down with it and we took it from him. Our rooms in the hotel were placarded, warning others of the disease and forbidding entrance.

After this long winter of sickness, Mother resolved to take Willie and myself to the seashore for the summer so we could recuperate. Through friends she heard of Miss Dudley's delightful boardinghouse at Annisquam, Massachusetts, but this lady had no room for us. We secured accommodations at a recently built hotel nearby where the rates were reasonable. This hotel was run by a tyrant, who strongly resembled the overseer in *Uncle Tom's Cabin*, and his wife, who took no pains about the food. Of course, we did not discover this until we got there and it was too late.

But lovely people came to that hotel, among them Mr. and Mrs. Wheeler from Buffalo with their son and daughter. Jane Wheeler was several years my junior, but Tom Wheeler and my brother were the same age and became fast friends. Tom visited us every summer after that for years, no matter where orders took us.

We had great fun in Annisquam. Salem Gibraltars were the popular candy that summer, and one crotchety old gentleman offered Leon Ballard, a noisy child, five Salem Gibraltars if he would keep absolutely quiet for ten minutes. The candies were about the size of a bar of chocolate and very hard to chew.

Mother

I remember a Miss Dorothy Van Patten, a tearing belle with many suitors, all of them trying to win her favor. We felt especially sorry for a Mr. Marder, who could secure no room at the hotel and spent the night on a couch in the sitting room. "She won't have me," he remarked gloomily to Tom Wheeler and Willie.

There was bathing at the neighboring beach and Mother tried it once but could not stand the chill of the water. One dip and I was warm all over. I spent some time on the beach once with a family of little children. I was teased about this by an admirer, Bennie Shute, who used to write me letters on birchbark. Sad to be honest, but I did not care for his attentions. The boy I hoped would be my husband was Charlie Chase. I met him but once, one day when I was passing a pleasant house facing the water. Though our meeting was brief, his looks and perfect manners won my heart and I made up my mind on the spot that he was the boy for me. But alas, Charlie died during the following winter and my romance was ended.

Eventually, after a number of weeks at Annisquam, the time came to go home. Mother, who was a delightful traveling companion, took us by way of Salem where, on a shopping trip, we bought a tiny witch, and she said:

> "This wicked old witch that here you see
> Was hanged by the neck to a great gallows tree,
> So we took her down and they sell her here
> For a five-cent Salem souvenir."

We visited Concord and Lexington, too, and best of all, Boston, where Mother took us to the Public Library to see Edwin Austin Abbey's superb murals of the Grail. So large were they that they were terrifying. We stayed at the Parker

House overnight and then started for Bethlehem. Father met us at the station. He had stayed at his post the entire summer, not joining us as he had at Sorrento. No doubt our summer of fun had been expensive.

The fall passed uneventfully for Willie and for me, but before the year 1897 was ended, Mother, to her utter amazement, found that a new child was on the way. Willie was then twelve, and no child had been born in the meantime.

Convinced that she was too old and would die, Mother went to the best doctor in Bethlehem, Dr. Wilhelm, who assured her that she was fine. But Mother did not want the baby to be born in the hotel, and in those days women did not go to the hospital to have a child. The baby was expected in July, and with new orders likely to arrive at any minute, our parents did not know quite what to do.

Then, in early summer, Mother had a piece of good fortune. One day in town she happened to meet her cousin, Agnes Colby, who lived on Fountain Hill. Agnes explained that her husband, Albert, was threatened with tuberculosis and she was taking him to Saranac Lake in New York State, while her mother and two young children went to stay with her brother. Out of a clear sky she said, "So you can have the house and our two good maids for the summer and your baby will be born in comfort."

Of course our parents closed with this wonderful offer and gladly paid the rent. Soon after July 4, Willie and I were sent off to Carlisle and left in Auntie's charge while Ammah came to be with Mother. I don't know why we were banished to Carlisle, for we were not noisy children. It may have been a lack of space. But I know I was homesick and longed for my friends.

I was delighted to see Ellinor Hays again. One day she brought us an invitation from Mrs. Moore. Marianne Moore, her brother, and her mother were storybook people to us and we were thrilled. Honey's tact was remarkable, as she knew Auntie had a great fear of water, be it ocean, bay, or creek. "Mrs. Moore is taking her children for a picnic on the creek, Miss Rose. She and Warner will do the rowing; she has invited me and she hopes you will let Laura and Willie come too. She will provide the supper. They are not going far," quoted Honey.

Wonderful to relate, Auntie said we might go. I cannot remember Marianne's saying anything, but Mrs. Moore read us the "Three Golden Apples" from Hawthorne, and the picnic was a huge success as Warner was always most companionable and he and Honey were friends of long standing.

Years later, when Marianne and I had become real friends, I remember being asked to breakfast in their garden. When I arrived, I saw a neat little pot hung over a small fire and in it was a breakfast egg for me, as my hostesses did not care for eggs. Mrs. Moore went busily in and out of the kitchen, making the coffee and bringing out the rest of the breakfast. Presently she called to her daughter, "Are you watching Laura's egg?"

Marianne replied in doleful tones, "It's been in and out so many times I don't know what it's like now."

Her mother was horrified but I cared not at all what state the egg was in when it was finally produced. I was blissfully happy just to be there.

In due time, on July 22, 1898, a telegram came addressed to me. It said:

Arrived today. Mother doing well. Tell Aunt Lizzie.

Mother with Stephen Vincent Benét, aged four weeks

And it was signed: "Stephen Vincent Benét."

A letter followed. It could only have been composed by Father.

> My dear Sister:
> Mother I am really very fond of already. The old man says, "I am the child of his old age." My mother thinks

I am too sweet. I heard her say so. Thank heaven, here comes afternoon tea and I need it in my business. Goodbye my dear sister.

It was at least three weeks before we went home and saw the new member of our family in his cradle. So minute and tiny he looked! Of course, being maternal by nature, I was greatly pleased. Willie, I think, was much disappointed, though later on he was devoted to Stephen.

Willie and I were delighted to be back. Father had already gone on to Buffalo, our new station, and he composed the poem that terminated the Bethlehem chapter in our lives:

BALLAD ON LEAVING BETHLEHEM

Soon Jim and Martha Yochum
Will miss their desk mates dear,
Their callous friends will joke 'em
When they drop the unbidden tear.
Farewell to Estes, Duncan,
And the Merrimans and Sayres,
Can Buffalo such true chums show?
No, there they put on airs.
Farewell to Ethel, Mildred, Ruth,
To Sally M., that heart of truth,
To Jean and Anna, O, what woe,
We must depart for Buffalo!
Farewell to the Eagle, that hostelry regal,
Where happy we lived on the third story high,
Where William grew pallid on too much shrimp salad,
And Laura had measles and wanted to die.
Farewell to Olive Williams, to Cornelia and to Bess,
To Norman, Ned, and Amory. We long their hands to press,
The seven Williams children. It makes us want to bawl,

When we think of Wentworth, little dear, the youngest
    of them all.
Our song's of little worth and the meter, it is various,
But you musn't want the Earth, our position's most
    precarious,
For the orders they have come and we really do not know
When we'll have to make things hum
On the road to Buffalo.
The orders have come! Yes, the orders have come,
Poor Laura is weeping and William looks glum,
Their home will be henceforth in far Buffalo,
And Bethlehem's pleasures no more can they know.
The M.P.S., our teachers kind,
In deep distress we'll leave behind,
Farewell to Vogel, Wunderling,
Towards Buffalo we bend the wing.

CHAPTER SEVEN

Buffalo

BEFORE we left Bethlehem, Stephen was christened by Dr. Allen in water from the River Jordan, brought back by an admiring friend. William and I were the godparents and Mary Lee Rose, our cousin, an additional one. Named for the beloved grandfather who had died three years before, Stephen was a unique individual and, even as an infant, blasé. Mother said that she would catch him looking at her with the strangest expression, as if he understood all those things that we were making such a fuss about. Father once remarked:

> "With his snapping eyes and his turned-up nose,
> He's a strange melange of Benét and Rose."

But Stephen satisfied him and became in a way his favorite child.

Stephen was barely two months old when his travels began.

Mother, Willie, and I, with nurse and infant, went to Ammah's in Carlisle for a short spell until Father should find an abiding place in Buffalo. He sent us colored postcards and word that a house he had been offered possessed a chute for the flour barrel. We had hopes. But that house was abandoned in favor of a small but comfortably furnished one on Parke Street, directly opposite the Franklin School, where, however, we were never enrolled. Our capable parent had engaged two maids and when we arrived they were waiting for us. Sadie, a Canadian, proved a very good cook. Mary Potter, an English girl who had had some nurse's training in London, became Stephen's devoted nurse. To our joy, Ammah went with us to Buffalo for a visit.

Since Grandmother Benét always paid for my schooling, I was enrolled at St. Margaret's, the best girls' private school in town, but Willie was less fortunate. The school that his friend Tom Wheeler attended was expensive—too expensive. So Willie went to the State Normal School, which he never liked.

We had good neighbors in Buffalo, the Sedgewicks, with two little girls, who lived next door. But on the other side, the family of Doothers was peculiar. Winter came, and Buffalo abounded in snow. One day, walking home from school, Willie and Tom Wheeler drew legends in the snow with their sticks. With no personal animus, they happened to mark on the Doothers' front steps, "Funny doings," as they had marked several other stoops with similar comments.

The next morning, Mother was summoned to the parlor. An unexpected visitor had arrived—the elder Miss Doother, in a blaze of wrath.

"We were greatly insulted," she began, "by the message

your son dared to print on our steps, 'Funny doings.' Did you know of this escapade, Mrs. Benét?"

"Indeed! Certainly not," said Mother. "I am very sorry you should have been annoyed. It was a childish piece of mischief but I assure you he meant no harm."

"No harm!" sniffed Miss Doother. "Perhaps you are not aware that my father holds a greatly respected position in this city."

"But you see," Mother replied, "do excuse it, for it was thoughtless but not intentional."

"We do not suppose that you or your husband did it."

"Hardly, Miss Doother." Mother in her turn was getting annoyed. "We do not amuse ourselves in that way. You shall have an apology—and now I really must go to my baby." Politely but firmly, she ushered the enraged spinster out. The apology followed and this ended the episode.

The only member of our family the haughty Doothers ever acknowledged after that was Stephen. Mary wheeled him to the park daily when the weather was good and nearly always passed their house. The Doothers, sitting on their front porch, probably wondered how such a depraved family had ever acquired such a beautiful baby.

William got the most fun out of Buffalo. He met all Tom Wheeler's friends—Roswell Parke, Leighton Lobdell, George Sicard, and more. They formed a club and secretly read detective stories which were frowned upon by their families. Father was much amused by discovering Frank Merriwell, the popular hero, concealed by William under cushions in the window seat.

Recalling my year at St. Margaret's School, I think on the whole it was a pleasant experience. I especially enjoyed my

Stephen and doll, George Dewey, in Buffalo

friendship with Alice Van Arsdale, and there was another charming girl, Mildred Register, daughter of a downtown rector, who was much beloved. There were disadvantages, too. I could never draw and we were expected to illustrate certain compositions. I cannot remember what happened in arithmetic, though I always excelled in English and history. But I was never one of a "set," as my brother was, because of his friendship with Tom Wheeler. Although his sister Jane was much younger, I was entertained at their home at a delightful Halloween party. But St. Margaret's never had the place in my heart that the Emma Willard School occupied later on.

Mary Lee Rose, now eighteen, visited us that summer and Father entertained her by taking her with him on his various inspection trips. They saw Niagara. I was only fifteen and didn't count, so deep down I must have been a little jealous. Anyway, I had decided to become a nurse.

Then our life was upset by Stephen's illness. He developed "summer complaint," lost much weight, and the doctor came almost daily. Fall had set in before he finally recovered.

The expected orders on the Government's part set us again in motion, as there was no use to renew the lease on the comfortable house that belonged to Mrs. Curtis for the short time before the move. When the inventory was taken and all breakages replaced, Mrs. Curtis complained that the "skeleton" was missing. Concealed in some dark closet, we thought! Discovered at last, the skeleton turned out to be a tiny object, not as long as a spoon, which had been bought at the dime store.

We emigrated with baby and nurse to Mrs. Strong's boardinghouse on Delaware Avenue, where rooms were spacious but meals a total loss. Our friends and playfellows were all in school and how we longed to join them! We became thoroughly bored while we waited.

During these last days of our stay in Buffalo, we had paired off in the rooms—Father and William occupied a double bed in one room, Mother and I were housed in another, and Mary Potter and Stephen in another. We had not been warned that the bed in Father's room was a folding one.

Willie, Mother, and I were spending the evening together

and she, as usual, was entertaining us by reading aloud a wonderful book, *The Cloister and the Hearth*. We were at that exciting chapter where Gerard outwits the robbers, when, to our horror, Mother and I saw that Willie, who was lying stretched out in the bed, was slowly but surely rising toward the ceiling. We flew to his rescue, sat firmly upon the bed, and managed to bring it down to its original position. I believe the chapter on the robbers was finished eventually. Father missed all of this adventure.

It was while we were in Buffalo that we had a visit from Grandmother Benét. Although in delicate health, she yearned to see the baby, her husband's namesake. With Uncle Laurence as her escort, she crossed the ocean once more and made the journey to Buffalo. She brought Stephen many pretty things, and her meeting with him was touching. We were still in our house at the time of her arrival, and Stephen was standing up in the playpen when she entered the room. Although she was wearing deep mourning, he held out his arms to her, seeming to know she was a member of the family. She remained with us for a number of weeks, and Mother did all she could for her comfort. Grandmother Benét visited our schools and heard my report, which, fortunately, was a good one. During this visit Grandmama and Mother talked more intimately and drew closer than they had ever been.

There was a shock in store for our grandmother, as Uncle Larry soon afterward announced his engagement to Margaret Cox of Washington, a friend of years. When Uncle Larry came to take Grandmama back to Paris, she broke down. It was a final good-bye for all of us, and I think she knew it, though she talked of my "coming out" in Paris when I was a few years older.

CHAPTER EIGHT

Watervliet Arsenal

AT long last we turned our backs on Buffalo and Mrs. Strong's unappetizing meals. We had been lucky enough to draw Watervliet Arsenal, where the big guns were manufactured, as our next home. Mary, Stephen's nurse, stuck to us when we left Buffalo, for she was utterly devoted to her little charge, who was beginning to walk. With his bobby curls and sage remarks, Stephen rapidly became the pet of the Arsenal.

Situated across the Hudson River from Troy, the Arsenal was about four miles from Albany, capital of New York State. Both cities possessed fine schools, among them the Emma Willard of which Miss Knox was the principal, and the Albany Academy presided over by Dr. Henry Warren—a military academy which left plenty of room for literature and languages. Willie rode a trolley to his school, and I walked over the bridge

Two views of Benét home at Watervliet Arsenal

or took the ferry across the Hudson River to Troy.

My daily companions on the way to school were the Hobbs girls, Eleanor and Marian, and Elizabeth Kent. Although Eleanor was fifteen, just my age, my true friendship was given to her younger sister Marian, a lovely child of twelve. For some reason, Elizabeth Kent, a general's daughter, and I disliked each other at once. In later years when we became close friends she told me she had often hidden in the bushes rather than walk to school with *me*. However, she was Stephen's friend and admirer from the time she first saw him in his carriage up to the end of her life.

I got on well at the Emma Willard School, except in the despised arithmetic. Helen Haight, the Latin teacher, not long out of Vassar, was a delightful girl and my great admiration. Fraulein Arnt, the German teacher, made her lessons a pleasure, and I enjoyed history and Bible history with Miss Lucas. Miss Jones who taught mathematics was my bête-noir, as Miss Lang had been at the Moravian Seminary.

Our youthful Stephen had become the fervent worshiper of his tall brother William, now fourteen, and as soon as he could speak plainly: "At's dear pretty Bubba," he would say, holding up a picture. Mother called him William's "little shadow." I was "Tissy"—but not in the same class until years later.

William did not return from school until three o'clock. On pleasant days, Nurse Mary would station herself on the lawn with the baby, to watch the horizon for the trolley from Albany. "Oh, there comes Brudder Willie," she would exclaim joyously. Well she knew that from then until Stephen's suppertime Willie would be caretaker and entertainer, amusing and devising games for the small brother.

When Stephen (who called himself Tibbie) was still in dresses, he discovered a ladder—quite a long ladder—that workmen doing some repairs had left against the side of the house. Before we older children who happened to be passing could catch him, he climbed like a small squirrel to the very top of the ladder, and no blandishments could budge him. Fortunately, Father appeared from the office, took in the situation at a glance and, grasping the culprit's skirts, bore him ignominiously down to earth. Stephen turned on his father: "Great Red Fox, Cousin Graylegs, thief and villain!" he spluttered, to our horror—Howard Pyle's *Wonder Clock* was popular in the nursery.

Mother, entering the nursery one morning, discovered an empty mousetrap and a dead mouse on the floor next to Stephen, who was holding a picture book. "What are you doing, dear child, with that dead mouse?" she asked.

"Oh, it isn't dead at all. It's a dear little mouse," replied her offspring. "I took it out of the trap this morning and read it a story."

A year or two later, on a warm summer morning, Stephen was busy with his soldiers on the front porch, murmuring: "The first platoon gets the first prize—'at's a red ribbon—and the second platoon gets the second prize—'at's a piece of brown bread," when Captain Horney, who lived opposite us and possessed a white rabbit, passed by on his way to the office.

"Oh, Tibbie," he said, looking over the porch railing, "those soldiers will never win a battle! Just look at that one with a broken gun!"

Stephen drew himself up. "It is my opinion," he announced firmly, "that he has a pocket pistol."

Stephen, five, opposite Captain Horney's house at Watervliet

As for Willie's school, in spite of the long journey back and forth, he was contented there and happy, and made many friends. But he was fearfully absent-minded. There was a saying that he had once appeared at drill with every piece of his equipment missing but his trousers. Later when his literary career was made, he became a tradition at the school and his poem on "The Old Brown School" was framed and hung up in the principal's office.

One day when starting for school in the rain, Willie asked if he might borrow Father's umbrella. "You may, my son," said Father, "but be sure to bring it back at three o'clock as I have an appointment with the Rotary Club in Troy."

Meanwhile the rain stopped, but knowing that Willie would be sure to forget the article in question, Father took his stand by the sentry box at the Arsenal's front gate. Just at that time each day the trolley coming from Albany to Troy met the one going from Troy to Albany. Willie was about to hop off his trolley when he caught sight of Father, and he promptly boarded the return trolley to reclaim the umbrella. Father chuckled, having known this would happen.

Another time when Mother was in bed with a sick headache, the maid brought her word that a boy from "Mr. William's school" was crying downstairs and said he "*must* see Mrs. Benét."

"Very well," said Mother wearily, and hurrying into a dressing gown, went to find out what was the trouble. The boy explained that the day before he had taken a valuable ring of his father's from its drawer without asking permission, had given it to Willie to hold while he was playing some game, and Willie had carried it home and returned to school that day minus the ring.

"You should never have taken your father's ring in the first place," said Mother.

"Yes, I know"—and he began to cry again—"if the ring is lost I shall be severely punished."

"Wait here," said Mother, "we'll turn out my son's bedroom." Every drawer was ransacked, the bed torn up, and the ring finally discovered between the frame of the bed and the wall.

The boy was humbly grateful. My mother noticed that the ring had a superb stone set in it. We learned that the boy restored it to its drawer in time and his father never found out.

Mother meanwhile gave up the thought of a restful morning. Why attempt a nap when excitement lurked in every hour of the day?

There was a golf course on our post and men from Troy would come by invitation to engage in their favorite game. The residents of Troy were well off and most hospitable, and officers and their wives at the Arsenal were frequently entertained by them. Because of the course, Father gave up his loved tennis for the time being and played golf instead. So did William, but I never cared for it. For some time Elizabeth Kent's friends, Julia and Mary Pattison, were afraid of me because she told them I read Latin for pleasure in the summer vacation!

It is my firm belief that Tibbie taught himself to read by street signs while in Carlisle with Mother on a visit to Ammah. On one occasion, Auntie was reading aloud to him from the book of Genesis and had just reached the fact that God took a rib out of Adam to make Eve. Stephen's eyes flashed. "That was a most inhuman act," he cried. "No man could live if such a thing were done to him." Stephen's interest in the Bible waned from that hour, although he confided with great pride that he himself had "guillotined a bug."

When we had been at the Arsenal a year, our compassionate mother invited Aunt Aggie's younger sister, Aunt Sophie, who had had a long illness and was, as we thought, convalescing, to come for a visit. The summer holiday was ending and Aunt Aggie had to return to her music pupils in Wayne, Pennsylvania, and our house boasted a good-sized guestroom. Then a tragedy developed. Aunt Sophie's illness became so serious that the post doctor got a nurse. It was not break-bone fever at all but cancer. For weeks poor Aunt Sophie lingered, her one pleasure visits from Tibbie. I was now sixteen and good at doing errands. I never remember one word of complaint

The only picture taken of the three Benéts when they were young

on the part of either parent and, when friends at the post would inquire, "And how is Miss Mahon, Captain Benét?" Father would reply cheerfully, "She is about the same and her recovery is slow, but we hope for better things." They took that illness in their stride. It terminated at last and Uncle Will Rose, Mother and Auntie's brother for whom Willie was named, came on to take charge of the burial in the family plot in Allegheny. I realize now how remarkable our parents were.

That summer the Wheeler children, Tom and Jane, invited us to Buffalo to the Sesquicentennial Celebration, and we had ten days of pleasure. Then it was time for me to put up my hair, and May Kent, Elizabeth's older sister, graciously offered to help me. I was very stupid about such things but I must have mastered the knot at last. Like my father, my feet were wonderfully swift but not my hands. The only picture that was ever done of us three children together was taken in Troy at this time, but I do not remember anything about it except that my dress was pink.

After our trip to Buffalo, the Wheelers paid us a return visit the following summer, and their stay was followed by one from Ellinor Hays of Carlisle. She made friends with everyone, the Hobbs and Elizabeth Kent, and we had numerous jaunts to Albany, and to Saratoga on a church picnic. The golf course fascinated Honey and she practiced daily, but Father said we were a staid sixteen compared with lively Jane Wheeler. After her visit to us ended, Honey went on to Rhinebeck where she had an uncle and cousins.

Fate was hovering to spoil our good times. It must have been at some point during the previous year that Mary Potter, Stephen's nurse, decided suddenly to leave us. Whether she was tired and wanted a change of scene or was in love, we never knew. But the cook said she departed weeping bitterly at leaving Tibbie. Our mother then tried several nurses, none of whom was satisfactory, and finally engaged one whose name was also Mary. In the fall of the year 1901, Mother decided to go for a week's visit to Brooklyn, the home of a favorite cousin, Martie Pattison. She planned to go Christmas shopping with Martie.

While Mother was away, Mary, on her afternoon off, visited a friend in Watervliet whose child had scarlet fever. We believed that she transmitted the germ to poor Stephen, who was about three and a half. What misery resulted. We older children with Father were banished to an empty set of quarters opposite; we could not go to school and were in quarantine. Mother, who had returned home, and a nurse remained in our house during Stephen's dangerous illness, from which he finally emerged peevish and unlike himself.

During his convalescence, Mother asked him what he would like for Christmas. He said, "A typewriter."

"Well," she remarked, "that's a pretty big present for a little boy like you."

"But so was our Savior," Stephen replied.

With his curls cropped off, Stephen looked like a picked chicken when he was borne over to the other house, that our house might be fumigated. Mother, nearly exhausted with the long nursing, was greatly vexed that Father had accepted a dinner invitation in Troy. But they went off in the post carriage, and Mother, who always looked charming in black velvet, was quite the belle of the party and enjoyed her dinner partner. Father was placed opposite. Their host was wealthy, and a different wine was served with each course. Father said later that he thought, "She (Mother) is not accustomed to this— she will be under the table presently." Nothing of the sort occurred and Mother said afterward the wine was like so much water.

Mother might have recovered more quickly from her long ordeal of nursing except that, in spite of all precautions, I took scarlet fever just after returning to school and catching up in my classes. I was seventeen and may truly say that those endless weeks back home in bed were one of the most unhappy experiences of my whole life. I did not like either nurse or doctor and that made matters worse. The one redeeming feature of that ghastly fever with attendant earache was, as usual, our precious mother. She had us all at home then, as William was suffering from a sore throat.

Every afternoon when the nurse went out for two hours, Mother appeared with a book and read aloud to me. We went through the letters of Princess Alice to her mother, Queen

Stephen about 1903 in the breech of the nation's first 16-inch gun which was developed at Watervliet Arsenal

Victoria, and then began George Eliot and finished volume after volume. I remember Tibbie appearing at the door, peering in to see me with a white stuffed animal in his arms. "I've named it 'Fuzzy White,'" he said proudly, "because that was the name of a bear."

The summer after I recovered from that fearful bout of scarlet fever I spent some blissfully happy weeks at the "Beachcroft" in Gloucester with Auntie as chaperone and Ellinor Hays and her sisters, both single and married. Esther Porter from Montclair was there with her mother and brothers, and one of their friends had a sailboat. So we sailed and had Ping-Pong games, all being the same age and delightfully inconsequent. How I hated to leave!

When school days were once more in session, everything was sadly changed. Miss Knox had resigned to take another school and Miss Leach took her place. All my loved teachers were gone and strangers presided in the classrooms. Miss Jones of the hated mathematics was the only survivor, she being a friend of Miss Leach.

I could not master the required mathematics and used to return home and dissolve in tears, while my small brother pranced gaily about, shouting, "You'll have to drop out of the class!"

Mother wrote quite a stiff letter to Miss Leach, stating that she could not tolerate the fact that on the eve of graduating my school work should end in "defeat and humiliation." Miss Leach, like the catty person she was, passed the letter to Miss Jones, who then attacked me. She told me that Mother had sent a dreadful letter, and that she was forced in self-defense to give me extra help for some time.

Meanwhile, Willie was taking part in public speaking at

school and whenever he rehearsed at home, stating that a certain great man "was a welcome and an honored guest," Stephen, like a small parrot, would state after him that so-and-so "was a welcome and a *hungry* guest."

It was in Watervliet when he was about fifteen that William's talent for verse began to show itself. He wrote a poem on harvesting with the refrain: "Reap on, ye harvesters, reap." This was published in *St. Nicholas*, paid for, and, to our intense surprise, translated into French.

Soon there was another poem, more dramatic:

> Far from a castle gray,
> Shining in the light of day,
> Rode a knight of the order gray,
> Fast!
>
> "Now by my faith," he cried
> As he dashed his sword aside,
> "By St. George and king," he cried,
> "I'd have saved her!"
>
> But no time to waste and now
> By the light from the old black scow,
> He saw through the rising dust, a speck.
> Larger and larger it grew,
> Until in the morning's hue
> A knight was seen in view.
> Riding fast
> And swift as an arrow to rest
> In mid-rib of the eagle's breast
> Sprang the knight to his steed's brown crest
> In the dawn.

Despite imperfections, there was the sense of rhythm William always possessed, whether dancing, skating, or canoeing. Willie was very like Mother in that he had her physical magnetism. He also had a sweet disposition and was always very popular with older people, especially the aunts. When he grew up his landladies always adored him. It is strange that such a sweet-tempered person as he developed such a terrible temper on occasions when he was older. While he would lose his temper violently, his anger was cold. Willie always was for the underdogs. He stuck up for them on all occasions.

At one time, two lines of a cherished poem he was writing at Watervliet caused a long and hot argument with Father. Willie had written:

> The ghostly maples gently sway
> And beckon with their shadowy boughs,
> As through their leaves the night wind soughs.

"Oh," said Father, who had been called in as critic, "that last word is pronounced 'suffs.' How would this be?" And he declaimed:

> "The ghostly maples gently sway
> And beckon like departing toughs,
> As through their leaves the night wind suffs."

But William was obdurate. Among his New Year's resolutions, recently made, was one: "Not to stand Father's teasing."

Both William and I graduated while we lived at Watervliet, and that was the end of childhood for us. Tibbie's of course continued for some years.

CHAPTER NINE

Benicia Arsenal

ORDERS for Rock Island Arsenal, Illinois, arrived rather suddenly in 1904. Mother shed tears and said she did not want to go to Rock Island, her sole reason being that a friend's only son had contracted some disease there that had paralyzed his legs. However, the orders could not be changed. Father never asked for favors, and it was finally agreed that Mother, with Stephen, should go to Carlisle on a visit to Ammah until our new quarters were ready. Father would go on ahead to Rock Island and share bachelors' quarters with another officer, while William, now often called Bill, and I returned to Yale and Vassar respectively.

The break-up at Watervliet was really sad, as we left many warm, lifelong friends, especially the Kents. "A great light has gone out of the Arsenal," said Mrs. Kent.

The visit to Carlisle was disastrous for Stephen. Though

there were no other cases in the town, poor Tibbie came down with typhoid fever. It was not recognized as such by Dr. Bender, Ammah's physician, who was getting old. It was Mother who helped Stephen through the crisis, by her prompt action saving his life. She spent the nights of Stephen's illness on a cot beside his bed, getting no real sleep but dozing fitfully. On one particular night she noticed that his breathing was strange and irregular. Picking him up, she threw up the window and held him there in the icy, winter air, calling out to Uncle Mont to get the doctor at once.

Dr. Bender came in a few minutes but did not seem to know how to cope with the situation. At one point, Mother shook the old gentleman by the shoulders and cried, "This child is dying. Do something, quickly."

The doctor gave her some pills to place on Stephen's tongue, and after a while they seemed to relieve the symptoms. Mother said, gently but firmly, that she wanted another opinion and so a Dr. Schwartz was called on the following morning.

Dr. Schwartz identified the disease as typhoid and said, "Mrs. Benét has taken her child through the crisis and now all that is needed is to nurse him back to health. I shall send a nurse tomorrow to help."

So Mother began to get some rest and Stephen to convalesce. But his recovery was slow, as this was his second serious illness within three years and he was a nervous wreck.

Then something very unexpected happened, and Mother never had to go to Rock Island after all. The Chief of Ordnance gave Father his first command—Benicia Arsenal, California! The following spring, 1905, we emigrated there in a body, Aunt Aggie joining us, as she was now a permanent member of the family.

"On the road Benicia way"

The trip West—the Royal Gorge

The Benét home in California

I think that overland journey and the places Stephen saw were the basis for the love of America and the outstanding patriotism that he developed later. We passed Great Salt Lake and other historic spots en route. Father met us at the station in Benicia and took us home to a superb house, really a mansion, with a garden and fountain at the back and an avenue of pepper and eucalyptus trees. Roses were everywhere, and later there was a hedge of sweet peas. There were rooms for everyone, and enough furniture to make us comfortable until ours arrived. We enjoyed the first meal that we had there—hot tamales that Father had procured for us.

This chapter really belongs to Stephen, his sayings and doings as he regained his health in Benicia. Mother said he sometimes ate as many as seven oranges a day from the tree in the garden. He lived in the open air and sun, for we found the summer climate wonderful, just cool enough. Here we acquired a dog, Prince, who adopted us, and also three horses, Nettie, Bird that William rode, and Chappell, my sweet-dispositioned mount.

Tibbie wrote me a birthday card that June, which accompanied my present, a brooch in the shape of a horseshoe:

> This pin, please wear for good luck's sake
> It comes from Nettie's toe,
> And never, never let it break
> Or where would Nettie go?

Stephen rides behind a guest on old Nettie, August, 1906

Laura, Helen Rockwell, Margaret Thompson (in white), and Stephen in sunny California

While William and I were home on vacations with our young friends, we tried always to include Stephen but could not take him on riding parties while he was still so young. He once generously offered the entire contents of his piggy bank when we needed some change, and Margaret Thompson, Kathleen Norris' younger sister who was visiting us from San Francisco, wrote:

> There is nothing tinhorn about Tibbie
> He's OK and A No. 1,
> From the time that he first left his cribbie
> He has lent us the whole of his mun.

We, of course, repaid him later.

Except when we had guests who brought children, Tibbie's

only playmates at Benicia were General and Mrs. Bellinger's four sons who came out with her every summer from San Francisco and occupied a vacant set of quarters. The two younger ones were just Tib's age. But they were not present when Tibbie was invited to a birthday party that took place next door. Much younger children had been asked from the village of Benicia which was only about a mile away. Stephen came home early from this party.

"Did you have a good time, dear?" Mother asked.

No reply.

"Wasn't there a birthday cake?"

"Yes," replied Stephen in tones of deep disgust. "They had a birthday cake, which was usual. But they didn't cut it, which was *un*usual." The little girl's parents were known for their economies, so the children at the party had been served small iced cakes while the large cake was reserved for the older guests.

Mother wanted Tibbie to spend even more time out of doors, and in the spring of 1906, McDonnell, our Irish driver, brought news of a donkey and cart to be bought at a reasonable figure. At first Mother planned to drive Stephen about the Arsenal herself. But after she had been thrown out once by that stubborn animal, Teddy, one of the soldiers in Father's detachment, Haney, was assigned the duty as driver for a certain length of time each day. At last Mother could relax, satisfied that her child was getting enough fresh air and sun.

After several weeks, Mother had a caller. A resident of Benicia, whom Mother did not know, came to the door, and Mother welcomed her cordially. The caller seemed shy at first but finally blurted out: "Mrs. Benét, your little boy has a donkey and cart and a driver?"

Stephen and the donkey in the avenue at Benicia. Mother stands by.

"Oh, yes," said Mother happily. "It does my heart good to think of him in the fresh air."

"Yes," returned the guest. "But you see, several of us neighbors felt you should know that the donkey and cart stand outside the principal saloon each day for an hour at a time with *nobody* in the cart."

"Oh," said Mother brightly, "it must have been some other child's donkey. Mrs. Smith, we have a reliable man as a driver. He wouldn't leave my son alone."

"No other child in Benicia is the possessor of a donkey and cart," answered Mrs. Smith firmly. "No doubt they wish they had. You will pardon me, Mrs. Benét, for bringing up the subject, but we thought you should know."

"Oh, I am grateful," said Mother gravely.

Poor Mother! All her dreams about her child's welfare gone with the wind! She felt she must question Stephen, but how? He was no telltale.

So she asked him tentatively, "Tib, Haney never leaves you alone, does he?"

"He has to get his lunch," replied her son in ominous tones.

"He gets his lunch free at the barracks," said Mother, "before he comes to take you out."

Driven to the wall, Stephen said, "He likes his beer."

"Does he take you into the saloon with him?"

"Oh, yes." A ray of happiness broke over Stephen's face. "He gives me change and I play the slot machine."

Sad to relate, this was the end of the daily drives. Haney, of course, lost his job. He had counted on Stephen's not telling on him. Without Haney's salty companionship and the slot machine, Tibbie lost interest in the donkey and I think the animal was finally sold, which was regrettable as he was to have been featured in a garden party Mother had intended to give for the church.

And then it was April 18, 1906, and the earthquake came. William and I were away at college at the time but of course we heard all about it. We were terrified until we received a telegram from Mother—"We are all well and safe." Actually, little damage was done to Benicia Arsenal except to the chimneys, a few of which fell down.

Tremors continued for some time, even after William and I came home for the summer. For several days after the quake the family sat in the living room all night, afraid to go upstairs. After two or three very uncomfortable nights they all went to their rooms but left the doors open so they couldn't jam if another severe quake came.

Mother and Father visited the devastated area, taking their lunch along with them. They sat on the curbstone to eat it—"Everything," said Mother, "goes here now." Not far from where they sat, a tremendous fissure ran through the street. One family we knew lived on white wine and walnuts for a day or two until they could obtain more food. Another family came to stay at our home at the Arsenal for a time, as they had been badly frightened by the disaster in San Francisco. The whole side of their hotel had swayed out as if about to fall, then swayed back and regained its position. For many days Mother contributed food to the refugees on the endless trains going east.

Because there were no children at the Arsenal during our stay there, other than the Bellinger boys in summer and occasional guests, Stephen was quite solitary when William and I were away at school. Our parents played with him to help occupy his time—I remember hearing about one game, called "Animal Pecularities" by Father. Grown-up visitors often joined in this game, too. "You should have seen your mother impersonating a seal," Father told me once. "She'd dive right off her chair." Our dear long-suffering mother would do anything to help amuse her youngest.

Stephen often went to the village church in Benicia with Mother, and he was usually quiet and attentive. But on one occasion, at the eleven o'clock service when the organist was hurrying through a hymn, he was so restless that Mother finally asked him what was wrong. "Nothing," replied Stephen, "only I don't like to hear the *Te Dum Laudamus* sung to ragtime."

There was one object made by Tibbie's adored brother Bill

Mrs. Laurence Benét—Aunt Margaret—on the lawn during a visit to Benicia with Stephen, Mother, and Father
Below: Father, Aunt Margaret, and Mother (left) view the Pacific at Coronado Beach during a trip to San Diego.

William and Laura at Benicia

that I do not think any family but ours ever possessed. Bill fashioned a robust tree with many limbs out of cardboard. It was called the "Miff Tree," the word meaning quarrel or disagreement. Each member of the family's Christian name from Father and Mother down was given a Miff, a bit of white paper marked "Miff." The tree stood ominously on the hall table. If, for instance, Bill and Father had a slight dispute over

Colonel James Walker Benét

some poem, their Miffs were tied to a low branch. If Mother and I disagreed over the color of some new dress, our Miffs were placed on a higher branch. But if a violent quarrel took place between Bill and myself, that was "Grand Miff" and we were exiled to the top of the tree and gazed upon with disdain by the rest of the family.

I think Bill's tree must have sometimes been used in a

William on Bumper

different capacity, for I remember on Stephen's ninth birthday that Bill hung clues to the location of the presents on its boughs. One of the clues read:

> Happy birthday, Tib, to you,
> You're a bunny through and through.
> Just gaze along the well-marked track
> And you'll meet your fate—something small and black.

All the other gifts were described thus by verses compiled

Tom Wheeler, Stephen, and William (seated) on the steps at Benicia

Laura (center) with a cousin and his wife at Benicia Arsenal

by this clever older brother, who in the younger one's eyes could do anything.

All this time Tibbie was reading, reading, and finally Mother took him to an oculist who put glasses on him at once and said he must wear them permanently. He was only nine or so at the time. Father had an excellent library and any book was available to his small son. Which ones Stephen had been browsing in goodness only knows, for he appeared at the lunch table from the library one day, turned to Father, and said gravely: "In the event of William's dying without issue, what do *I* do?"

"We'll talk about this later," replied his startled parent.

It was during our stay at Benicia that Stephen acquired a midget typewriter. On it he wrote three short stories. "Mr.

Stephen with a small cousin and Prince, the water spaniel

A "riding party" at Benicia. Stephen in sun hat in foreground.

Progg's Conversion" went like this:

>Mr. Progg reeled home from the saloon, singing as he drew near his house. His wife looked out of the window as he approached. "I will fix him," said she.
>
>Next day she went downtown and bought a cat, the duplicate of their pet cat. She also bought a can of green paint.
>
>That night when Mr. Progg again made his way home, singing "We won't go home until morning," a pair of fierce green eyes glared at him from the window of his little home.
>
>. . . . .
>
>An hour later a badly frightened man handed the pledge to his wife—and the cat understood.
>
>   The End

"The Butcher's Bill" was even more dramatic:

> Two men in cloaks and masks stood before the butcher's house and both had weapons in their belts. The first one spoke to the other.
> "I was about to be turned out of my house today, but he granted me a week's respite."
> Suddenly the shutters in the window above their heads were flung open. There STOOD THE BUTCHER.
> "Hands up," he said in the short sharp tones of one who has said it before.
> The men pointed their pistols at the window. The butcher started to spring out. The men sprang up in his direction. There was a flash, and the butcher dropped dead but not before he had fired two bullets.
> The next day they found them all dead, but clutched in the hand of one of those in mask and cloak was the BUTCHER'S BILL.

Unfortunately, "Philip Alabaster," the fine flower of Stephen's three tales done on his midget typewriter, is lost. The Philip of the tale was evidently a rué and the dangerous rival of the "I" in the story, who must have been Stephen himself.

As I remember it, Alabaster was apparently very fond of women, so his rival said bitterly, "I saw that I must beware of all women in future. But—we went into the woods and I was enchanted with her beauty. I married *her*. I began to entertain suspicions, however, that she was a part of Alabaster's vengeance. . . ."

And that is all that I can recall of this sophisticated tale. Anyway, Alabaster didn't take a knife to "I."

One time when Mother was on a visit to Carlisle, Stephen wrote her the following letter, on my best engraved stationery:

LB

My Dear Mother:—
Everything is going on finely

I mended my skates William is hauling wood down at Carmel Aunt Agnes is cleaning his closet, Laura is Prince is a little sick and sends love. Is everthin allright with you? How is Mark? Did the letter from Mrs Shayler reach you? The radish are half Dead aying "good-by" to Margery and Edward who are going to the city God's in his heaven all's right with the world" have have had my hair cut and much resemble a convict.

and one tomato-
is dying. The
Smallpox scare
is nearly over.
Raffles has been
caught by a young
artist. God bless
you all.
Devotedly
Tibbie

⊠ Prince his ⊞ mark

Laura as a bridesmaid on the porch at Benicia

Shortly after receiving this letter and returning to her family, Mother decided that it was time for Stephen to have some formal education. Father was averse to the plan, having himself suffered from terrific homesickness when he was sent away to boardingschool. But then he had been only nine and Stephen was now twelve. Mother was strongly in favor of it, especially because Stephen had no companions of his own age at Benicia Arsenal. Even William's and my friends had scattered, since Bill had graduated from Yale and was living in San Francisco studying shorthand and I, my Vassar education completed, was "out" enjoying a round of visits.

And so Mother prevailed, and Stephen, too, began to move out of childhood—a childhood full of warm memories because our unusual parents had made the years of growing up a constant and imaginative adventure for us.

Index

Abbey, Edwin Austin, 59
Albany, New York, 71
Alice, Princess (England), 81
Allen, Dr., 65
Annisquam, Massachusetts, 57, 59
Arnt, Fraulein, 73

Baker, Harris, 27, 30, 31
Baker family, 23, 27, 31
"Ballad on Leaving Bethlehem," 63–64
Ballard, Leon, 57
Belchertown, Massachusetts, 4
Bellinger, General, 91
Bellinger, Mrs., 91
Bellinger boys, 91, 94
Bender, Dr., 86
Benét, Frances Rose (mother), 1–5, 9, 11, 12, 14, 15, 17, 18, 20, 24–27, 29–36, 39, 40, 46, 47, 49, 50, 52–53, 55, 57, 59, 60, 61, 65, 66–67, 69–70, 74, 76, 77, 79, 80–82, 85, 86, 87, 91–94, 97, 102, 107

Benét, James Walker (father), 1–5, 9, 17, 22, 23, 25–28, 31, 34–36, 39–43, 47–50, 53, 55, 60, 62, 63, 65, 66, 67, 69–70, 74–77, 79, 80, 84, 85, 88, 94, 96, 100, 107
Benét, Laura
  childhood, 1–84
  education, 6, 27–30, 42, 43–51, 55, 66, 67–69, 71–72, 82, 84, 85
  illnesses, 57, 63, 81–82
Benét, Laura Walker (grandmother, Grandmama), 6, 8, 16, 18, 20, 22, 26, 38, 39, 54, 66, 70
Benét, Laurence (uncle, Uncle Larry), 6, 8, 22, 24–25, 54, 70
Benét, Pedro (great-grandfather), 18
Benét, Stephen Vincent (brother), 85–107
  birth, 61–62
  childhood, 73–74, 77, 84
  christening, 65
  education, 107
  illnesses, 69, 80, 86
  letter to mother, 102–107

nurse, 66, 67, 69, 71, 73, 79–80
poems by, 89
Benét, Stephen Vincent (grandfather, Grandpapa), 4, 9, 18, 26, 39, 65
death of, 53–54
Benét, William Rose (brother)
childhood, 1–84
disposition, 84
education, 27–29, 42, 52, 55, 66, 71, 75, 82–83, 84, 85
illnesses, 9, 11, 56–57
"Miff Tree" made by, 96–97
poems by, 75, 83–84
Benicia Arsenal (California), 85–107
Betge, Frank, 50
Bethlehem, Pennsylvania, 39–64
Bethlehem Iron Company, 39
Bird (horse), 89
Boston, Massachusetts, 17–18, 59–60
Bridesburg, Pennsylvania, 23, 30
Buffalo, New York, 63–64, 65–70, 71, 79
Buffington, General, 3–4
Buffington, Mrs., 4
Buffington, Eliza, 4
Burger, Ben, 46–48
"Butcher's Bill, The," 102

Carlisle, Pennsylvania, 11, 13, 14, 60, 66, 77, 85
Chappell (horse), 89
Chase, Charlie, 59
Child's History of England (Dickens), 30
Clark, Helen, 36–37
Clark, Miriam, 36–37
Clark family, 5, 36–38
Colby, Agnes, 60
Colby, Albert, 60
Conlin, Fred, 46, 48
Cox, Margaret, 70
Curtis, Mrs., 69

Davenport, Brewster, 19, 20
Davenport boys, 19
Dickens, Charles, 27, 30
Doother family, 66–67
Duncan, Bill, 55, 63

Earthquakes, California (1906), 93–94
Eliot, George, 82
Estes, Dr., 56

Estes, Mrs., 56
Estes, Jean, 56
Estes, Will, 55, 56, 63
Evangeline (Longfellow), 52

Fitzpatrick, Mrs., 44, 52
Fortress Monroe, Virginia, 2
Frankford Arsenal (Pennsylvania), 23–38

General Grant (Shetland pony), 38, 39, 40, 45
Grider, Mary, 45

Haight, Helen, 73
Hark, Dr., 44, 45–46
Hark, Anna, 45
Hark, Hilda, 45
Hawthorne, Nathaniel, 61
Hays, Ellinor Blaine, 14–15, 61, 79, 82
Hays family, 14–15
Higgins, Isabel, 47
Hobbs, Eleanor, 73
Hobbs, Marian, 73
Horney, Captain, 74

Ingersoll, Elaine, 20
Ingersoll, Enid, 20

Jenkins, Jim, 55, 56
Jenkins, Marian, 56
Jolly (dog), 26–27
Jones, Miss, 73, 82

Kent, Elizabeth, 73, 77, 79
Kent, Mary, 79
Kent family, 85
Knox, Miss, 71, 82

Lady of the Lake, The (Scott), 36
Lang, Miss, 45, 73
Leach, Miss, 82
Lear, Edmund, 22
Legron, Mrs., 11
Lobdell, Leighton, 67
Longfellow, Henry Wadsworth, 52
Lucas, Miss, 73

MacMullen, Ida, 42, 52–53
Mahon, Agnes (great-aunt, Aunt Aggie), 32–34, 77, 86, 103

Mahon, Montgomery (great-uncle, Uncle Mont), 11, 12–13, 86
Mahon, Sophie (great-aunt), 77, 79
Marder, Mr., 59
Merriman, Norman, 56
Metzger, Mr., 11–12
Metzger Institute (Carlisle, Pennsylvania), 11
"Miff Tree," 96–97
"Mr. Progg's Conversion," 100–101
Mitcham, Adelaide, 24
Montanya, Annie, 5–6
Moody, J. S., 20
Moore, Mrs., 13, 61
Moore, Marianne, 13, 61
Moore, Warner, 13, 61
Moravians, 40, 43–45, 53, 55
Murray, Maxwell, 36–37
Myers, Mildred, 52
Myers, Sarah, 42

Neill, Gertrude (great-aunt), 32
Neill, Kate (great-aunt), 13, 32
Neill, Sophie (great-aunt), 32
Nettie (horse), 89
Nonsense Book (Lear), 22
Norris, Kathleen, 90

"Old Brown School, The," 75

Parke, Roswell, 67
Pattison, Julia, 77
Pattison, Martie, 80
Pattison, Mary, 77
Pennsylvania Railroad, 12
"Philip Alabaster," 102
Pitman, Mrs., 26–27
Porter, Esther, 82
Potter, Mary, 66, 67, 69, 71, 73, 79–80
Prince (dog), 89, 104, 106
Putz, 53
Pyle, Howard, 74

Register, Mildred, 68
Rittersville, Pennsylvania, 40–41
Rock Island Arsenal (Illinois), 85, 86
Rose, Elizabeth Neill (aunt, Auntie), 11, 12–13, 60, 61
Rose, Frances, *see* Benét, Frances
Rose, Mary Lee (cousin), 65, 69

Rose, Mary Lee (grandmother, Ammah), 6, 8, 11–15, 53–54, 60, 66, 77, 85, 86
Rose, Will (uncle), 79

St. Nicholas, 27, 83
Sayre, Frank, 56
Sayre, Nevin, 56
Schwartz, Dr., 86
Schwartz, Mrs., 55
Scott, Sir Walter, 28, 36
Sedgewick family, 66
Shute, Bennie, 59
Sicard, George, 67
Smith, Mrs., 92
Smith, Deborah, 42
Sorrento, Maine, 16–22
Springfield Arsenal (Massachusetts), 1, 4–5, 9
Strong, Mrs., 69, 71

Thackeray, William, 28
Thompson, Margaret, 90
Troy, New York, 71, 72, 77

Uncle Tom's Cabin, 6, 36, 57

Van Arsdale, Alice, 68
Van Patten, Dorothy, 59
Very, Mrs., 8
Victoria, Queen (England), 81–82

Warren, Henry, 71
Washington, D. C., 9, 38, 39
Watervliet Arsenal (New York), 71–84, 85
Werlich, Percy, 57
Wheeler, Jane, 57, 68, 79
Wheeler, Tom, 57, 59, 66, 67, 68, 79
Wheeler family, 57, 68–69
Wilhelm, Dr., 60
Williams, Amory, 52, 63
Williams, Bessie, 52, 63
Williams, Cornelia, 52, 56, 63
Williams, Ned, 52, 63
Williams, Norman, 52, 63
Williams, Olive, 52, 56, 63
Williams, Wentworth, 52, 64
Wolle, Fred, 56
Wonder Clock (Pyle), 74

111

About the Author

LAURA BENÉT was born at Fort Hamilton on New York Harbor, attended the Emma Willard School and Vassar College, and now lives in Manhattan.

Some have writing thrust upon them. With two distinguished brothers, Stephen Vincent and William Rose Benét, Laura Benét at first decided to be a social worker and spent four active years with the Spring Street Settlement. Later, however, as reviewer and editorial assistant, she wrote for two New York newspapers. But family tradition prevailed, and she began to devote herself to her own work—the several volumes of poems for which she has become widely known and her many fine biographies.

A new book of poems, *Bridge of a Single Hair*, has recently been published. Many months of research went into a biography entitled *The Mystery of Emily Dickinson*. Of her latest book, a memoir of childhood, Laura Benét says, "I did not have to do research for this small book—only to set down on paper scenes I could recall that were vivid and even amusing."